Contents

Introduction to the Second Edition

The field of fabric decoration, now commonly called surface design, has seen a great deal of growth and development since the publication of the first edition of *Design on Fabrics* in 1967. The number of books and articles on the subject have increased, along with the development of classes and programs in surface design at all levels of education. The energy generated by this activity led to the establishment of the Surface Design Association in 1976. The purposes of this organization are diverse, but they all aim to promote surface design as a creative endeavor through communication. Since the establishment of the Surface Design Association, there have been numerous national and regional conferences and workshops on all aspects of surface design.

The present revised edition includes photographs of current work that indicate the excellence and diversity of the creative effort that is now seen in the field. Health hazards in the arts are a major concern, and information has been included and changes made in the text to reflect these concerns. New materials and technology have been made available in recent years, and these are also reflected in the current edition.

Coauthor Meda Parker Johnston died in 1977 after a long illness. Her death was a great loss to many of us in surface design, but her legacy is well established and will be felt for many years. This present edition is dedicated to the memory of Meda Parker Johnson.

Many people were helpful in making this revision a reality and I wish to extend my gratitude to all of them. Robert G. Stetson, ICI United States, Inc., has over many years provided the authors of this book and others technical assistance and answered many questions on dye chemistry in terms understandable to the craftsperson. His help has been greatly appreciated. Dr. Constance Chiasson, Purdue University, has also provided help with portions of this book dealing with dye chemistry. I extend special thanks to the artists, colleagues, manufacturers, suppliers, and students who have provided material essential to this revision.

Glen Kaufman
Athens, Georgia
August, 1979

Introduction

The subject of this book is the embellishment of fabric surface by means of dye or pigment: in a phrase, fabric decoration. Throughout its long history fabric decoration has made a significant contribution to the cultural heritage of countless civilizations, and it continues to be a dynamic force today.

The story of fabric decoration is a story of design. The two cannot be separated, but must be considered as one. We have not attempted to provide an outline in basic design, since excellent material on this subject is available in other volumes. Rather, an attempt has been made to relate generally agreed upon design basics to fabric decoration, with the hope that each craftsman working with the techniques covered in this book will develop his personal approach and achieve personal solutions.

Special emphasis is given to the materials and processes of fabric decoration with the desire that the craftsman understand their unique potentials, learn to control them, and use them to express his individuality.

Both the inexperienced and the practiced craftsman have been considered in the planning of this book. It is meant to be a guide in a way that suits each person.

It should be noted that a Glossary of technical terms has been provided.

A book of this nature is not possible without the help of many individuals, each contributing in a special way. We wish to thank the students who have asked many questions and provided many answers over the several years during which the book has developed. Many examples of their work illustrate the volume. Our appreciation goes to the individual craftsmen and manufacturers who have supplied information and photographs. It also goes to the outstanding museums that have been most cooperative in providing photographs of work in their collections. Special thanks are due to Alice Baldwin Beer of The Cooper Union Museum for her encouragement and complete cooperation, and to George Fuller for the line drawings that are included in the book. Finally, we are indeed grateful for the many valuable contributions our editor, Nancy C. Newman, has made.

1. History of Fabric Decoration

Origins of Fabric Decoration

From the earliest recorded history, man has decorated the fabric surfaces of his environment. Perhaps his clothing was decorated first, then other items necessary to his existence. Although it may be impossible to pinpoint the beginning of this art, it is obvious from the available evidence that it was an important development in cultures widely separated in time and geographic location.

Numerous attempts to explain the origins of fabric decoration have resulted in a variety of theories. It has been proposed that early cultures of hunters and planters evolved characteristic designs which were used in the hope of favorably influencing their lives, e.g. improving the hunt or crops. Decoration may also have served as a means of identification within and between cultural groups. Other designs may have occurred by accident, such as a hand- or footprint of mud or clay on fabric, and it is possible that natural materials such as leaves, twigs, or stones were used to apply a colorant to cloth.*

Whatever the origin of the earliest fabrics decorated with colorant, it is obvious that fabric decoration has been a significant and dynamic force in man's cultural history. Religion, economics, and psychology have been or are factors in the continued development of this aspect of the fabric arts.

While no decorated fabrics exist from the earliest known cultures, other artifacts indicate the existence of embellished surfaces. Archaeological investigations have brought to light a variety of stamps that may have been used for printing fabric in Mesopotamia 5,000 years ago. Some of the stamps that have been found are cylinder and rocker shapes, and others are flat with a handle on the back, indicating a variety of uses.

Other evidence of decorated fabric has been found in early civilizations of this culturally rich area. Babylonians and Assyrians used patterns in sculptured representations of clothing textiles. From cultures in this area the arts of fabric decoration spread and were adapted to their new environments, producing a variety of distinct styles.

Further indirect evidence of decorated fabrics is found in Egyptian mural paintings dating from as early as 2500 B.C. The motifs are geometric in design and are used in repeat, possibly the result of a stamping technique. No fabrics thus decorated have survived. Specimens of hieroglyphs painted on fabric dating from 1545-1350 B.C. have been found, as well as resist-painted and mordant-dyed mummy cloths from before 1000 B.C. This early activity was followed by block printing, described in historical accounts as early as the fifth century B.C., and the use of clay or wax resists combined with refined mordant dyeing. It is believed that some of these dyeing techniques traveled to Egypt along trade routes from India.

Pliny the Elder (23-79 A.D.), a Roman writer, described a complicated dyeing process in a section of his *Natural History* entitled "A Remarkable Process":

Moreover in Egypt they have a device to stain cloths . . . which they besmear not with colours but with certain drugs that are apt to drink and take colour: when they have so done, there is no appearance in them at all of any dye or tincture. These clothes they cast into a lead or cauldron of some colour that is seething and scalding hot: where, after they have remained a pretty while, they take them forth again, all stained and painted in sundry colours. An admirable thing, that there being in the said cauldron but only one kind of tincture, yet out of it the cloth should be

*W. Born, "Textile Ornament," *Ciba Review* #37, January, 1941, pp. 1322-26.

stained with this and that colour, and the foresaid boiling liquor change so as it doth, according to the quality and nature of the drugs which were laid upon the white first. And verily, these stains or colours are set so sure, as they can never be washed off afterwards.*

Asia

India, perhaps, has had the longest continuous history of decorating fabrics with dyes. Printing blocks dating from 3000 B.C. have been found; they form the foundation on which the rich fabric culture of the country has been built. Indian printed cottons and silks have been marketed throughout the world and have had great influence on both the economy and the aesthetics of many countries. No other country has had so strong an impact on the history of dye-decorated fabrics.

Records dating from 400 B.C. indicate that colored chintzes were common. The word "chintz" is derived from the Hindu *chint*, meaning colored or variegated. The Greek physician Ctesias, writing of India about 400 B.C., alluded to resist-dyed and hand-painted fabrics. Early colors may have been made with fruit, flower, root, or bark stains that were made fast by the addition of acid soil or mud containing iron. Out of these early procedures grew the now complicated chemistry of dyeing.

In 327 B.C., when India was invaded by Alexander the Great, colorful printed cottons were again described by the Greeks. As a result of such invasions and the establishment of trade routes, printed and painted Indian cottons became known in the wider world of Asia and beyond. In the second century A.D. Arab traders brought Indian printed cottons to Europe via the Red Sea. Two centuries later, Indian merchants and sailors who settled in Java introduced wax resist techniques which developed into the highly individualistic "batiks" of that area.

A significant number of Indian fabrics has been recovered, many of them from the ruins of Fostat (Old Cairo), Egypt. They date, roughly, from the twelfth to fifteenth centuries A.D. and give evidence of the lively trade between the two countries. Many of these fabrics were block printed with resist and dyed either with blue (indigo) or red (madder). The designs are striking in their directness and simplicity—qualities that grew out of the technique used. They are, for the most part, two-color prints consisting of the natural color of the cotton ground and either blue or red, some with tints of these colors resulting from several dyeings. As a result of the resist approach, the backgrounds were dyed

Resist block print on cotton, India, 14th-15th century. Found in Fostat, Egypt. (Courtesy of The Cooper Union Museum)

Resist block print on wool , India, 15th century. (The Metropolitan Museum of Art, Gift of V. Everit Macy, 1929)

darker in color than the motif, which remained the lighter color of the ground cloth.

When Vasco da Gama discovered a sea route to India in the sixteenth century, Indian textiles had assumed a more intricate and exotic quality which quickly attracted the interest of the Europeans. For a number of years Portuguese and Spanish traders had a virtual monopoly of the distribution of Indian calicoes both to other Asian countries and to Europe. Calicoes were named after the seaport of Calicut in southwest Madras from which many were exported. In the late sixteenth century, with the establishment of the British East India Company, other European traders imported the Indian cottons to a growing market in the West. This brought about great changes in the production of printed fabric in Europe.

The designs of the calicoes contrasted sharply with the earlier resist prints. The fabrics were brilliant in a wide variety of fresh colors, and the motifs

* Philemon Holland (trans.), *The Natural History of C. Plinius Secundus* (Carbondale, Illinois, 1962), p. 427.

employed were complex, often without definite repeat. Flowers, plants, trees, and vines in fine detail were combined with animal and sometimes human figures, with exotic polychrome effects. The individual pieces frequently contained a large central motif (e.g. a fantastic tree growing from rocks or earth inhabited by peacocks and other fauna) surrounded by a border of flowers, small trees, or trailing vines. These fabrics were used as bedcovers, valances, or wall hangings rather than for clothing.

The techniques employed were as complicated as the designs and required a comprehensive knowledge of dye chemistry to achieve brilliant and lasting results. A Jesuit priest, Father Coeurdoux, described a method of decorating cottons in letters dated 1742. Following is a brief summary of his account. First, the cloth was prepared by a bleaching and mordanting process using an extract of a dry fruit called cadou and buffalo milk. The design was then applied to the fabric by pouncing charcoal dust through a perforated paper cartoon. Next, the design was outlined with a brush using black iron and red dye. Indigo was used for blue, and all areas not to be affected had to be covered with wax before dipping in the blue dyebath. Then the wax was removed, the cloth washed and mordanted again, and other colors applied. The process was repeated for each color that was added, with areas waxed to preserve colors already applied. Father Coeurdoux gave detailed accounts of each operation and descriptions of the specific plant or mineral materials used for each color.*

The eyewitness account gives a clear idea of the mastery these craftsmen had over the intricate dyeing process—a mastery that was long envied in Europe and that was approached there only after decades of experimentation. It was the Indian painted calico that set the standards of design and technical achievement for many years after its arrival in the West.

Some years after the Indian printed cottons first found a receptive market in Europe, strong influences were felt that had detrimental effects upon their design. As a result of the great demand for calicoes, methods had to be altered to shorten the production time. Much of the hand painting was replaced by block printing, and designs were simplified by utilizing repeated motifs. Europeans placed special orders requesting the inclusion of family crests and armorial bearings commemorating spe-

Coverlet or hanging, painted and dyed, India, 18th century. (Courtesy of The Cooper Union Museum)

Painted and dyed cotton, India, 17th century. (Courtesy of The Cooper Union Museum)

* MacIver Percival, *The Chintz Book* (New York, n.d.), pp. 10-12.

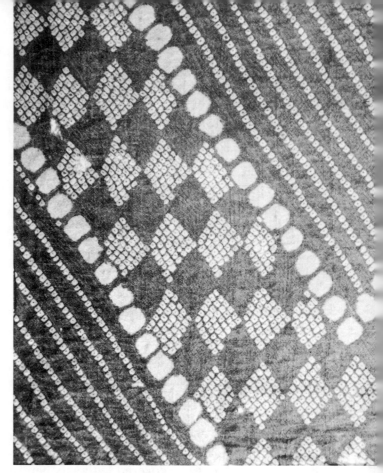

Sari, tie-dyed cotton, India, ca. 19th century. (Courtesy of The Brooklyn Museum)

Tie-dyed silk, Japan, 16th-17th century.

cial events, and the designs on the fabrics began to change from their original indigenous character to incorporate extraneous elements and motifs.

In addition to the painted and printed fabrics that became known in many areas of the world, there were other traditional Indian techniques that were employed in the embellishment of cloth surfaces. One that was highly developed but found little interest among Europeans was tie-dye, or *bhandana*, in which sections of the fabric were bound tightly before dyeing, creating a design through resist. The effects achieved with this approach were generally abstract, unlike those of drawing or painting with which Westerners were familiar. The technique was also difficult to imitate. The one exception may have been the bandanna handkerchief, ornamented with white spots on a blue or red ground, which was developed by the Europeans.

Early in its history, China developed sophisticated cultures in which fabric decoration was a significant art. Block printing is thought to have originated as early as 400 B.C., and further developments in fabric printing took place during the Han Period (206 B.C.-220 A.D.). The techniques of silk weaving and embroidery were also highly developed in China, and they overshadowed approaches that utilized dyes and pigments for embellishment. The latter techniques, however, as well as weaving, were introduced to Japan beginning in the third or fourth century A.D. and became highly developed national arts in their new environment.

Few fabrics exist from the primitive age of Japanese cultural history, although there is some indica-

tion of simple geometric ornamentation on clothing from the evidence of terra-cotta tomb figures. Not until the eighth century A.D. did Japan produce a variety of decorated fabrics, and much of it was a result of Chinese influence, which reached a high point in the T'ang Period (618-907 A.D.). Frequently the importation of fabric prototypes from China resulted in frustration, because the technology needed to adapt them to Japanese use was lacking.

During the Nara Period (710-784 A.D.) in Japan, however, fabric was decorated with stamped, painted, and stenciled patterns, and the technique of wax resist was used. A unique method called jam-dyeing was also employed. The cloth was folded in two and jammed between two wooden boards that were perforated in a design, and dye was poured on the perforations.

The decorated fabric was used primarily for clothing (this has been the case up to recent times), and the designs consisted of symmetrical patterns or regular repeats of the same motif, with polychrome effects.

About the twelfth century the kimono began to develop as the national dress of Japan, and new types of decoration, characterized by large-scale, free motifs, were used to embellish it.

Between the fourteenth and sixteenth centuries foreign influences again had a great impact on Japanese fabric decoration. The importation of fabrics from China during the Ming Period (1348-1644) led to more experiments with graphic designs that could readily be realized with dye work. Motifs utilizing flowering plants, flowers and birds, and animals were developed and refined in painting and stencil work. These pictures drawn on fabric used for clothing showed no feeling for the relationship between patterned surface and the function of the fabric.

Another strong influence on Japan in the mid-sixteenth century was that of the Indian calicoes introduced by Portuguese and Dutch traders. The Indian printed cottons were popular with the upper classes primarily for their use as linings or undergarments; the poorer classes used them to cover small boxes and other items. The calicoes revealed an entirely different approach to Japanese craftsmen. The designs were suggestive rather than literal, abstract rather than realistic. The scale of the designs was frequently much smaller than that employed to decorate the kimono.

Stencils for printing textiles, paper, Japan, 1615-1867. (The Metropolitan Museum of Art, Gift of Clarence McK. Lewis, 1953)

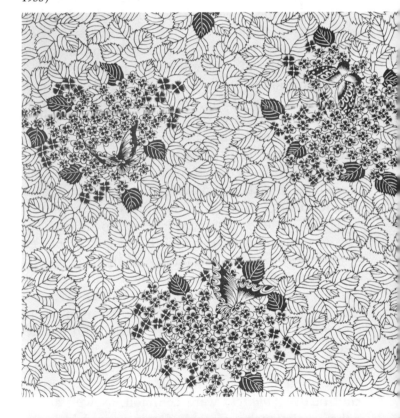

Two types of fabric were produced in Japan as a result of the importation of Indian cottons: hand-blocked prints in indigenous colors and designs, and hand-painted copies which were of poor quality because Japanese dye technology was inadequate.

In the Edo Period (1673-1801) Japanese craftsmen developed numerous decoration techniques. Among these was starch-resist dyeing, which was used to decorate the kimono in free designs. Since the style of the kimono was established by custom, one was distinguished from another by its embellishment. This led to an endless variety of designs, and seldom if ever were any two exactly alike.

A part of Japan that produced distinctive techniques and designs is Ryukyu, a group of fifty islands (including Okinawa) 400 miles south of the main Japanese islands. Although somewhat isolated from the mainstream of Japanese culture, Ryukyu had periodic contact with China, Korea, and parts of Southeast Asia.

Stencil dyeing was highly developed and used in combination with resists and hand painting. Natural dyes known elsewhere were native to the islands: indigo, cochineal, and other plant and mineral ex-

Sarong, batik on cotton, Java, 19th century. (The Metropolitan Museum of Art, Gift of Mrs. John Stemme, 1919)

tracts produced a wide range of colors. Techniques and designs were used and refined over many centuries in Ryukyu, but they were considered primitive compared to methods used in Japan proper.

As noted earlier, Indian traders introduced resist dyeing techniques to Java about 400 A.D. These were developed over many centuries into a unique decorative technique commonly known as batik. In batik hot wax is applied to a fabric which is then dyed; the wax is removed, and the design revealed. A characteristic line or edge results from this technique, and in some pieces a unique crackle effect is realized by controlled manipulation of the waxed cloth before or during dyeing.

Four general types of resist techniques were developed in Indonesia: the application of rice-starch paste with the fingers, sticks, or leaves; bamboo stick batik, in which wax and resin are spread on cloth with a stick; the use of the tjanting, a special tool consisting of a handle and a reservoir with a spout or spouts, to apply hot wax; and the use of the tjap, a metal stamp, which is dipped in hot wax and printed on cloth.

The dyes used were limited in color range, the most common being indigo, which produced variations of blue, and rich browns. Other colors were used later, but the outstanding fabrics were created in a few colors with subtle variations.

The decorated fabrics were used primarily for sarongs, the native dress, and the designs employed a variety of indigenous motifs. Geometric motifs were dominant and were combined with representations of plant or animal life. The batiks were produced in limited numbers; cheap imitations were not made, and an active export market did not develop.

Other techniques were also developed in Indonesia, some of them combined with batik. Painting and tie-dye (*plangi*) were common, as well as another resist technique called *tri-tik*, in which the design was stitched on the fabric. The stitches resisted the dye, creating the design.

Sarong, batik on cotton, Java, 19th-20th century. (The Metropolitan Museum of Art, Bequest of Helen W. D. Mileham, 1954)

Child's dress, painted tapa, Celebes Islands, 20th century. (Cranbrook Institute of Science)

Europe

Fabrics from Asia and Africa were known in medieval Europe through travel and trade, but perhaps because dye technology was lacking, there was little attempt to duplicate the luxurious imported cloths. It was not until the eleventh century that there appears to have been any concentrated activity in fabric printing. Wood-block printing was developed in Germany for book illustration and as a cheap means of reproducing the designs of woven brocades, damasks, and velvets that were both admired and expensive. At first the blocks were small, but in time larger blocks were developed, and they increased production capabilities. The effort to imitate a woven fabric or subtle hand-painted cotton runs through the history of fabric decoration in the West for many centuries.

Since knowledge of dyes was limited in Europe, the early printers relied on pigments to embellish fabric surfaces. Black was frequently printed on natural linen ground as well as on colored fabric. Gum or some other sticky substance was printed to adhere gilding or silvering to fabric, creating some feeling of luxury.

Since the materials available were limited, the printers sought variety in motif to enhance their patterned cloths. The designs of German fabrics of the twelfth century show Byzantine and Near Eastern influences on subject matter and pattern. Pairs of animals were used, frequently with foliage, producing a free-flowing pattern. Other designs employed the same subject matter enclosed within pointed oval frames which were repeated, giving an allover effect. Stylized leaves, flowers, and fruits, as well as geometric motifs, were also copied from woven fabrics.

The art of fabric printing continued to develop and be refined through the sixteenth century. Designs became more complex and more detailed in pattern. As economic conditions improved, the demand for cheap printed imitations diminished, although it never disappeared. It was a propitious time for the introduction of a new stimulus to fabric printing.

As a result of the opening of trade routes to India, first by Portugal and then by other European countries, calicoes became available in Europe and were enthusiastically received. These cloths were called "pintadoes" and "indiennes" in Portugal and France respectively.

In 1631 the East India Company was granted permission to import the cottons to England, and they were an immediate success. There had previously been block printing on fabric in England, probably related to similar activity on the continent, especially in Germany. In 1676 William Sherwin was granted permission to print cottons by the Indian method using wooden blocks. Of course, knowledge of dye chemistry was limited, and the result was poor imitations of the originals. A method for printing flocking on silk, leather, and cotton as a cheap substitute for velvet, developed some years earlier, had had the same result. However, the wool and silk merchants were unhappy with the competition, and in 1700 the importation of Indian printed goods was prohibited. Despite the ban, the use of Indian calicoes and English copies increased and in some cases led to riots in which weavers and their supporters attacked women who wore printed cottons.

Block print, silver pigment on linen, Germany, 12th-14th century. (Courtesy of The Cooper Union Museum)

Block print, black pigment on linen, Germany, 13th century. (Courtesy of The Cooper Union Museum)

Resist block print on linen, Germany, 17th century. (Courtesy of The Cooper Union Museum)

Printed cotton, England, ca. 1820-30. (Courtesy of The Art Institute of Chicago)

Copperplate print on linen and cotton, England, ca. 1790. (The Metropolitan Museum of Art, Bequest of Charles Allen Munn, 1924)

Printed cotton, England, dated 1761. (Courtesy of The Art Institute of Chicago)

The business of printing flourished in England in the early eighteenth century as dye techniques and their application were mastered. Further efforts were made to prohibit the manufacture of calicoes, but freedom to print on pure cotton was granted in 1774. With this recognition of printing as a true industry came further development. In the 1770's the roller was introduced in fabric printing and greatly increased the output of the industry. It did limit the length of the repeat and the scale of design, however, and because of these limitations, block printing continued to be used for furnishings fabrics.

Another innovation in the printing industry that had a great impact on the design and production of fabrics was the copperplate, developed by Francis Nixon in Ireland about 1750. The designs were usually printed in one color (red or blue) on a natural ground. The motifs were complete "pictures" repeated in simple and obvious ways. The subject matter consisted largely of pastoral or classical landscapes, groups of figures or *chinoiseries* (what the English presumed to be Chinese). The designs reflected not only the fashions but also the events of the time—adventure on the seas, the excavation of classical cities, and military campaigns. It is not difficult to understand these sources of design as we witness similar reflections of interests and events in our fabrics in the twentieth century.

The printed fabrics with large-scale designs were widely used in home furnishings, while smaller patterns were employed for clothing fabrics. As the market increased, so did technical developments in the chemistry of dyes and the production of cloth. Industrialization of fabric printing continued in the nineteenth century and led to the revolt by William Morris in the 1870's.

Morris, student of architecture, poet, writer, craftsman, and avid socialist, was cofounder, with John Ruskin, of the Arts and Crafts movement. He worked in a number of crafts, among them fabric printing, and he stressed knowledge of the materials and the process as a means of humanizing the life of his time. His designs were largely based on nature. He wrote, "I must have unmistakable suggestions of gardens and fields, strange trees, boughs and tendrils. . . ."* Contemporary with Morris' last designs for printed fabrics were those of the Art Nouveau movement, which also had significant influence on the art of fabric decoration.

The introduction of Indian calicoes to France in the seventeenth century and the subsequent history of the fabrics follow very closely the developments in England already described. They became popular very quickly, were opposed by the weaving industry and prohibited, but managed to increase in popularity, production, and sales. The early copies of the Indian prints in France were accomplished with the

"Daffodils and Crocus," by Arthur Wilcock, roller print England, ca. 1890. (Courtesy of The Cooper Union Museum)

"Windrush," by William Morris, block print on cotton, England, 1883. (Courtesy of The Cooper Union Museum)

* Graeme Shankland, "William Morris Designer," in Asa Briggs (ed.), *William Morris Selected Writings and Designs* (Baltimore, 1962).

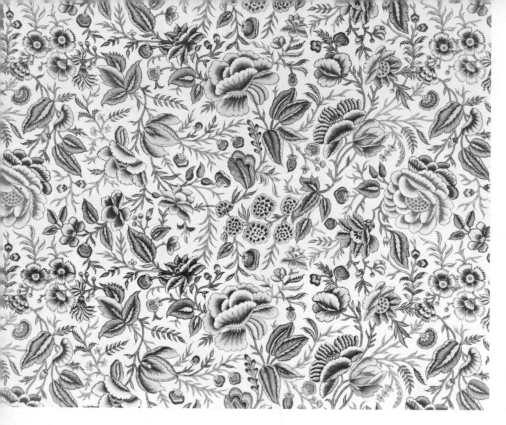

Block print, *Toile de Jouy*, France, ca. 1775. (Courtesy of The Cooper Union Museum)

use of pigments because the knowledge of dye chemistry was very limited. These cloths were not outstanding in design or in technical accomplishment.

The name of Oberkampf and the *Toiles de Jouy* he developed stand at the apex of French fabric printing art. Christophe-Philippe Oberkampf was born in Germany in 1738 to a family long involved in the dyeing and printing crafts. His father had worked for many years to develop a successful resist print method and in the 1740's achieved his goal.

Young Oberkampf traveled to France and worked in chintz printing. In 1759 he set up the historic print works at Jouy, a short distance from Paris. Oberkampf was responsible for the complete operation, from design to finishing of the cloth. The largest part of his production was single-color copperplate prints, the earliest in red dyes. By the end of the eighteenth century the business was thriving, and he was producing complicated designs in a number of colors, using both blocks and copperplates. Oberkampf traveled about Europe evaluating his markets, seeking new designs, and buying cloth. He received French royal sanction and patronage, which added greatly to his prestige and prosperity. Early in the nineteenth century rollers were employed for printing at Jouy, greatly increasing the capacity of the print works.

Oberkampf's success depended to a great extent on his ability to provide designs that were readily acceptable and on his use of inventions and innovations that had been developed elsewhere. He was sensitive to the particular tastes of the moment and was able to satisfy them on short notice. He frequently used *chinoiserie* designs. Later, peasant scenes and other pastoral themes dominated his work, followed by allegorical designs or designs based on mythology. Political events did not escape his attention: both the French and American revolutions provided subject matter for printed cloth. It was possible to change elements in a stock pattern to play upon last-minute developments in historical and political matters.

The effect of printing "pictures" was to create a delicate texture rather than a pattern on the fabrics, especially when they were draped. It was an approach to design that paid little heed to the final use of the cloth, and by present standards may be judged ineffective design.

There was other activity in the decoration of fabric in France. Abstract or floral motifs were repeated to create an effective pattern on fabric to be used in a variety of ways. Some of the more striking examples of this work were done with resist techniques in strong indigo blue, creating simple, direct, and positive designs. It was Oberkampf, however, who made the lasting impression, and whose original *Toile de Jouy* designs are available and furnish interiors today.

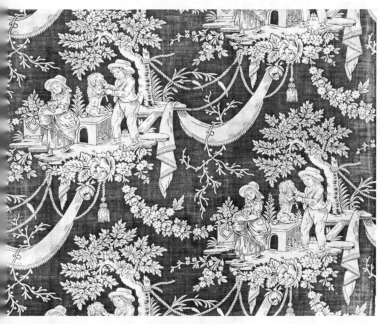

Resist print on linen, France, 19th century. (The Metropolitan Museum of Art, Rogers Fund, 1924)

Wood-block print on cotton, *chinoiserie*, France, 18th century. (The Metropolitan Museum of Art, Rogers Fund, 1924)

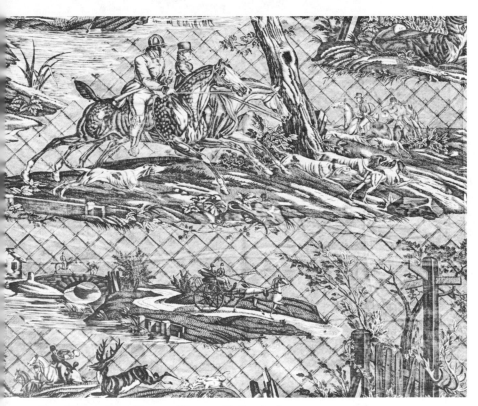

"La Chasse," by Horace Vernet, *Toile de Jouy*, copperplate print on cotton, France, 1815. (The Metropolitan Museum of Art, Rogers Fund, 1913)

Resist print on cotton, France, 18th century. (Courtesy of The Art Institute of Chicago)

19

Block prints on linen, *noboyka*, Russia, 16th-18th century. (Courtesy of The Brooklyn Museum)

Between the sixteenth and eighteenth centuries a significant group of prints known as *noboyka* (printed calico) were evolved in Great Russia. These fabrics were printed from wood blocks with vegetable colors on rough linen. Other fabrics of this period, upon examination, appear to have been printed with pigments. They were used for clothes, vestments, standards, tents, curtains, tablecloths, and bookbindings. The first printers were probably painters of icons who were familiar with the decoration of flat surfaces. Later, special groups of craftsmen traveled from village to village printing fabrics to suit the needs of the market.*

The unique quality of these prints is a directness and simplicity that grow out of an honest utilization of the wood-block technique. The prints show an understanding of the potentials and limitations of the technique. Much of the design quality is a result of the mark of the tool cutting the wood surface, which gives a fresh and spontaneous look to the work. The motifs are frequently based on floral, geometric, or pictorial themes, with a repeated design creating a flowing pattern.

L'Art Rustique en Russie (Paris, 1912), p. 10.

Resist stencil print with cassava paste on cotton, Nigeria, 20th century. (Courtesy of The Cooper Union Museum)

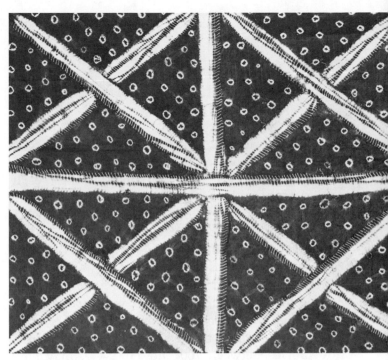

Tie-dye, indigo on cotton, Nigeria, 20th century. (Courtesy of The Cooper Union Museum)

Africa

A number of fabric decorating techniques have long been used in the cultures of central Africa. The first decorated fabrics were probably painted directly with the fingers or a simple brush. The motifs fall into three general categories (more than one may be combined in a single fabric). There are those that tell a story, those that have symbolic significance or that serve as identification, and those that are simple ornamentation with a pattern.

Fabric printed with a plant-leaf stencil or stamps made of stick or sections of calabash is also found. The fabric printed with calabash, made by the Ashanti of Ghana and known as *Adinkra cloth*, generally consists of a variety of stamped designs repeated in a rectangular grid. Some of the motifs fit together in an allover repeat, while others are more isolated.

Tie-dye is also used, especially in Nigeria, to create strong, simple designs of a geometric nature. Printing with resist pastes has a long tradition and is done effectively with indigo, occasionally incorporating crackle effects.

Block print, tar on dyed cotton, *Adinkra cloth*, Ghana, Ashanti, 20th century. (Courtesy of The Cooper Union Museum)

The Americas

In the Americas the cultures which play the largest part in the history of the fabric arts are those of pre-Columbian Peru. The craftsmen of these early civilizations made outstanding contributions both in fabric structure and ornamentation (needlework and color application). Various Peruvian civilizations separated by time and geography practiced fabric decoration with dyes and pigments in techniques which were similar, yet developed independently. Among these painting and tie-dye were primary.

Although there is no proof as yet, it has been suggested that some of the repeat motifs used to decorate fabrics between 700 and 1100 A.D. may have been executed with hand stamps, rollers, or primitive stencils which have been found. However, few if any fabrics exist which indicate beyond doubt that such devices were used.

Many of the examples of painted fabric that exist today indicate that the craftsmen had a feeling for and an understanding of motif repetition to create an effective surface pattern. The motifs are frequently enclosed in rectangles and make use of negative and positive areas to create the over-all design. The designs include abstract and stylized animals, birds, and human figures, as well as geometric shapes. They are frequently done in designs of one color on fine cotton, while other examples utilize a variety of colors, giving a more complex effect.

Tie-dye was used as a decorating technique on closely woven fabrics and open gauze weaves. Some designs were carefully controlled repeats, while others were more random and free in approach. One method which was unique to Peru incorporated tie-dyed stepped triangles arranged in a patchwork, creating a repeat design of intriguing complexity.

Later South and Central American cultures used stamps and rollers for decorating fabrics. Indigenous groups in the Americas, from South America to the northwest coast of Canada, employed techniques of hand painting on a variety of fabric materials or substitutes such as leather and hide, though none reached the excellence of the Peruvians. After the Spanish conquest, many Peruvian techniques were used to produce fabric designs dictated by the Spanish.

Painted cotton, Peru, 1100-1400. (The Textile Museum, Washington, D.C.)

Painted cotton, Peru, 1100-1400. (The Textile Museum, Washington, D.C.)

22

Tie-dyed alpaca(?), Peru, Tiahuanaco Period, ca. 700-1100. (The Textile Museum, Washington, D.C.)

Painted shirt, Peru, Chimu Culture, ca. 1100-1500. (Courtesy of The Brooklyn Museum)

Wood-block resist print on cotton, United States (?), 18th century. (The Metropolitan Museum of Art, Gift of Norman M. Isham, 1933)

Printed cotton, United States, 19th century. (Courtesy of The Art Institute of Chicago)

In 1770 calico was first printed in the United States by John Hewson of Philadelphia. The process and designs were direct imports from Europe, for immigrants brought their trades and skills to America. The American industry grew gradually, and by 1811 there were printers established in Philadelphia and New Jersey, which became printing centers, and in other locations. However, many printed fabrics were imported from England and France to meet the demands of the American market. Special commemorative designs were rushed to American merchants while the events were still fresh and the subject matter meaningful.

There is now some doubt about the origin of many prints, especially indigo resists, that were previously thought to be of American manufacture. There is little that was distinctive enough about American design or production in the eighteenth and early nineteenth centuries to make positive identification possible. It was not until the twentieth century that American technology and design made a unique contribution to the field of fabric decoration. Especially significant was the development of screen printing, today widely used by industry and handcraftsmen.

Contemporary Decorated Fabric

Color-decorated fabrics produced by industrial and hand methods are making a vigorous and dynamic contribution to our cultural milieu. The need for patterned surfaces seems to be increasing as a reaction to the post-war Modern style that has been a strong influence since the late 1940's. The clean, precise, and sometimes austere quality of the Modern style is being replaced by or juxtaposed with surfaces that are richly embellished and highly expressive of the individual.

Fabrics, lush in color and surface texture and decorated with a myriad of motifs, are available to enrich the environment. All categories of apparel and commercial and residential interiors make increasing demands upon the producers of decorated fabrics to fill the growing need. When the demand is great, the thought and planning that go into development of the product are frequently minimal. Watered-down copies and quick translations result. There are, however, designers for industry and artist-craftsmen whose concern is with quality in design and execution. The results of their concern provide the illustrative material for this section.

In order to fully appreciate the development of decorated fabrics in our era, a familiarity with the technological advances since 1900 is useful. The screen process method of printing was patented in England in 1907 and about twenty-five years later was successfully adapted to commercial uses. Much of the early work in this technique was limited to printing on paper and felt, the latter used for banners. Since this printing utilized inks or pigments rather than dyes, the fabrics produced were stiff of hand; they were suitable for drapery fabrics but seldom for apparel. Developments in the use of dyes altered this situation after 1940.

Although the procedure of forcing dyes or pigments through a screen stencil has remained basically unchanged, the speed and ease with which it is accomplished have been greatly improved. Where hand methods are employed, procedures for ensuring correct registration and movement of screens and the squeegee have been refined. However, fully automatic screen printing is now widely used by industry. In this method the screens remain stationary while the fabric moves under them, receiving any number of perfectly registered color prints. The printing capacity of these machines ranges from 100 to 400 yards per hour.

Roller printing is still widely used in commercial printing, but the technique has limitations, especially in the size of the repeat. Photographic techniques are now used in place of the old hand methods to transfer a repeat to the roller, greatly reducing the cost of producing a new design.

Prior to World War I most of the commercial dyes available to the American market were produced under European patents. Because they were unavailable during that conflict and again during World War II, American companies were forced to develop a diversity of dyestuffs. As new fibers were developed, too, dyes were required to color them, and at present there are over 1,500 dyes available in this country. In 1956 the fiber-reactive dyestuffs were introduced, providing craftsmen with dyes that produce bright colors of excellent fastness and may be applied with relative ease.

The designs of many of the outstanding decorated fabrics produced commercially and by handcraftsmen seem to have certain characteristics in common. There is a healthy concern for the potentials of the materials and processes of decoration techniques, leading to constant investigation and exploration. Design grows out of the materials and processes in a natural way. Fewer realistic drawings and paintings are imposed upon printing techniques. A freer approach, emphasizing rich color and flowing pattern, is resulting in fabrics which possess unity of design and are suitable for a variety of uses.

A sound relationship is evolving between handcraftsmen and the industries related to fabric decoration. Industry utilizes design ideas developed by craftsmen and adapts them to production methods. Industry also employs craftsmen to develop new concepts relating design to materials and processes. The craftsman, on the other hand, utilizes the technical developments in his own studio work. These interrelationships between creative individual craftsmen and the designing-producing-marketing complex are subtle and intricate. They are, however, necessary for a continued positive growth in the field of fabric decoration.

Developments in the dye industry, in education, and in communication over the past decade have given a dynamic vitality to surface design. New dye technology has become increasingly available to the craftsperson and has been used to create a body of work that demonstrates a strong personal expression. Wall hangings, quilts, wearable art, and soft sculpture are some of the important areas that have been strongly influenced by the processes and materials of surface patterning and color enrichment. Spontaneity inherent in some forms of direct application as well as the more studied effects of screen-printed patterns have developed simultaneously. Combinations of processes aid in the expression of a personal vision.

In the 1970s and 80s the strong creative thrust toward the enrichment of fabric surface with lush color and expressive pattern is in the hands of the studio artist, who uses these resources to stunning effect. The available technology has meshed perfectly with the desire to explore surface in challenging and dynamic ways.

"Reflection," by Elenhank Designers Inc., screen print.

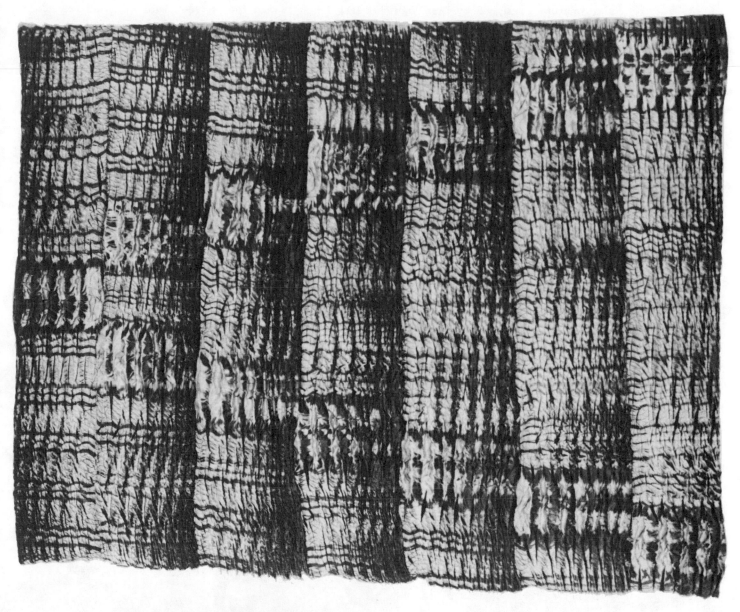

"Nightfall," by Pamela Scheinman, tie-dye (discharge) on black satin, 43″ × 55″.

"Mad Ludwig I," by Ed Rossbach, Color Xerox transfer print on weft, brocade weave, mixed fibers, 5½″ × 5¾″.

27

"Primavera," designed by Don Wight for Jack Lenor Larsen Inc., screen print on cotton velvet.

"Countryside," by Elenhank Designers, Inc., screen-print panels.

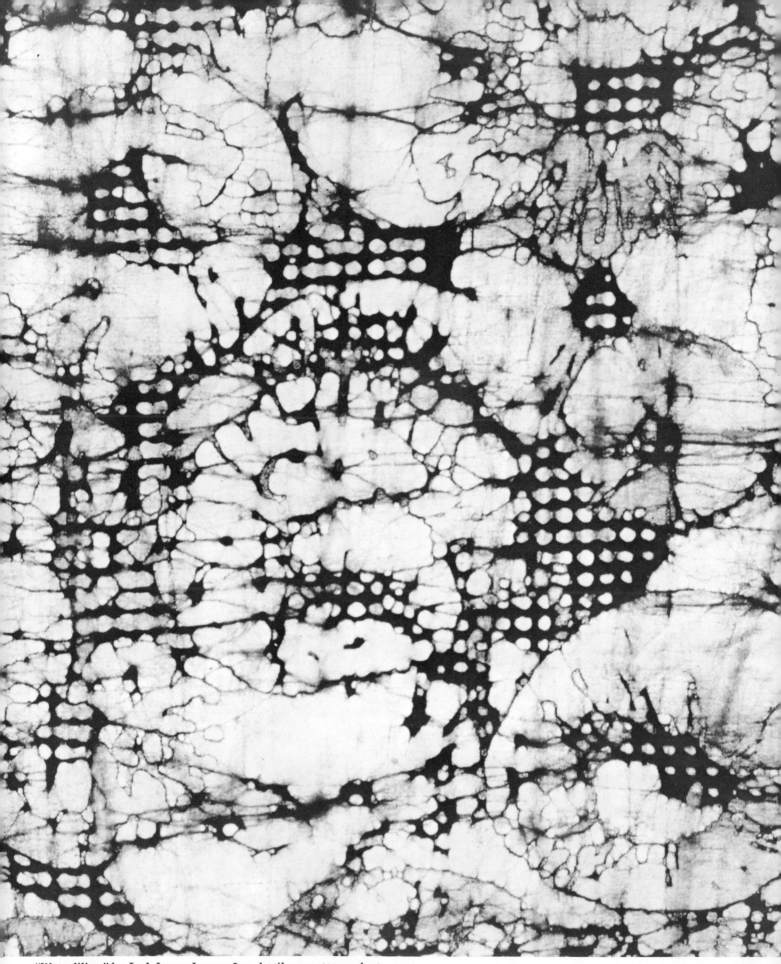

"Waterlilies," by Jack Lenor Larsen Inc., batik on cotton velvet.

"Mimosa," by Boris Kroll Fabrics, Inc., screen print.

"Steps and Shadows," by Zoë Woodruff Lancaster, screen print.

"Dunbar," by Cornelia Breitenbach, screen print and airbrush, dye and pigment, fiberglass-backed panel (detail).

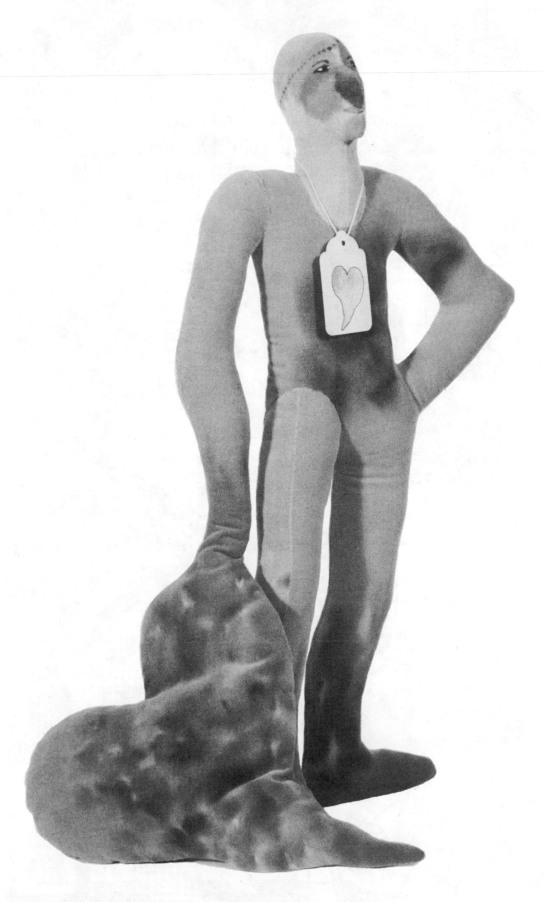

"Man with Heart I," by Lenore Davis, direct application on cotton velveteen, sewn, stuffed with embroidery, 21″ tall.

"Out of the Mud Grows the Lotus," by Katherine Westphal,
transfer print on panné velvet, quilt, 84″ × 60″.

"Beast in the Jungle," by Frances Butler, screen print.

35

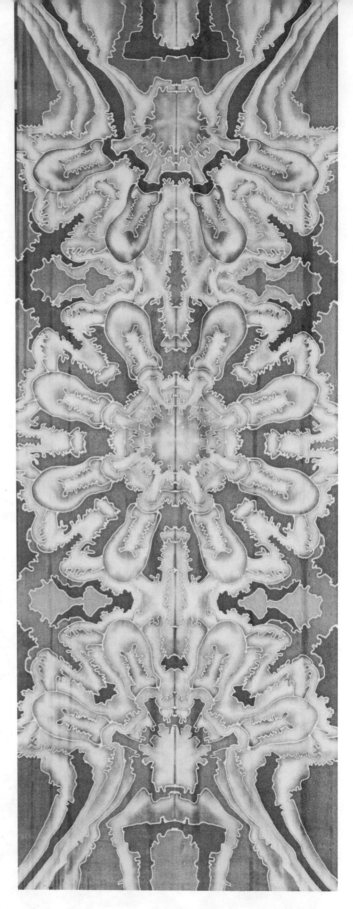

"Victorian Symmetry," by Ed Lambert, wax resist and direct dye on silk, 84″ × 120″.

"Pair of Indian Ikat Gloves," by Glen Kaufman, Color Xerox transfer print on cotton, 7½″ × 11″.

"Fans I," by Pamela Scheinman, screen-print discharge on
black satin, quilted and pleated, 60" × 45".

Tie-discharge and dye on cotton, by Meda Parker Johnston.

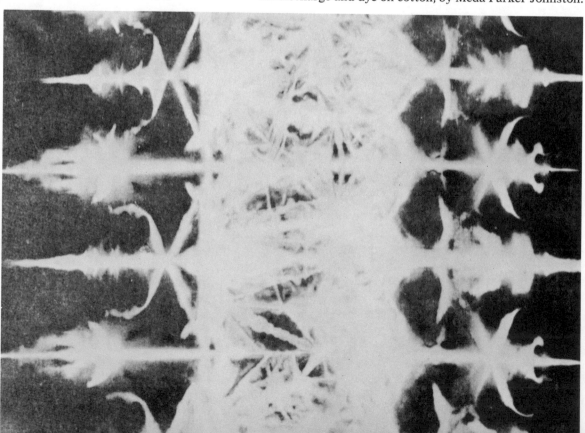

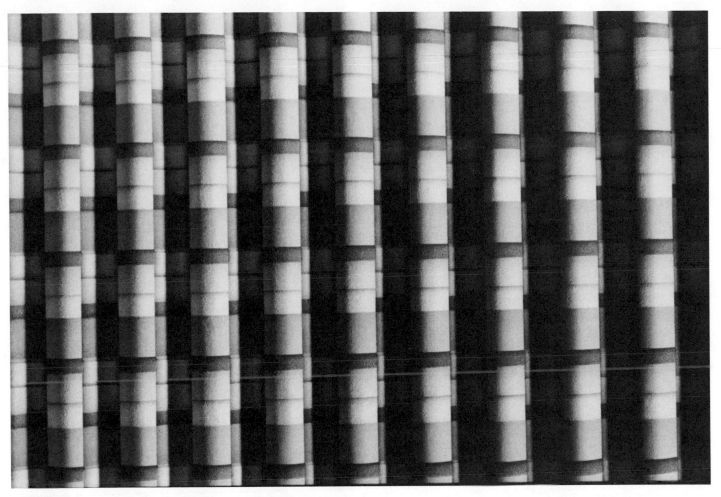

"Ellsworth," by Cornelia Breitenbach, screen print and airbrush, dye and pigment, fiberglass-backed panel (detail).

"Insects," by Frances Butler, screen print (detail).

2. The Criteria of Design

Good design, like good painting, cooking, architecture, or whatever you like, is a manifestation of the capacity of the human spirit to transcend its limitations. It enriches its maker through the experience of creating, and it can enrich the viewer or user who is equipped to respond to what it has to say.*

Design, in its broadest aspects, affects all phases of our lives today. It is an attitude, not a process or a product. In this volume our primary concern is the relationship of design to the fabric surface in a non-structural way. It is our purpose to encourage the craftsman to reach his own meaningful design solutions by increasing his awareness of his past heritage and his present environment.

It is not our intention to provide a complete experience in basic design in this chapter. We do wish to describe those aspects of design which relate specifically to fabric decoration. The elements of design and the principles by which these elements are applied are basic. Neither of these sets of concepts is the magic answer to good design. Rather, they provide a common basis for discussion and a point of reference. The use of them is not always clear but, more often, they must be subtly interrelated to produce an effective design.

Why decorate fabrics? The answer is a simple one. Decoration serves as a foil to plainness, to relieve the boredom of unembellished surfaces. Though the answer may seem obvious, the solutions to the design problems posed are not. Design for the surface of fabric presents special problems that must be understood if effective results are to be achieved. This does not mean there are ironclad restrictions or few possible solutions.

One unique aspect of fabric surface pattern is that it frequently is not used as designed. The flat, single-plane patterned surface may be draped in an interior or on a human figure, cut up and reassembled in a variety of ways, that is, used on curved surfaces or three-dimensional forms. The surface design is thus distorted from its original state on the single plane. This is the first important principle the designer must realize. A design should work well in a number of situations. Of course, some fabrics can be designed for a specific use, with room for few or no variations. These cases are rare. We see upholstery

*George Nelson, *Problems of Design* (New York, 1957), p. 13.

fabric used effectively for apparel, and dress fabric applied as wall covering. The designer cannot assume responsibility for every use his fabric is put to, but he must realize the possible uses and design with them in mind.

Elements of Design

Line has been described as a series of connected spots and as a moving point. As a moving point it can suggest motion in a variety of ways. A line may be rectilinear or curvilinear, and if it meets itself, it can enclose a space, creating a shape. A line has a very personal quality that grows out of the materials and the individual manipulating them. Each individual and each material has unique qualities that contain great potential for a variety of lines. It is of the utmost importance to fully understand the significance of this potential. Each of the decorating techniques described in later chapters possesses potential for certain unique types of lines or edges. Visualize, for example, the lines created by a knife cutting film, a brush trailing blockout, a gouge moving through linoleum or wood, a cord tightly binding fabric, and a tjanting tracing a flow of hot wax.

Lines possess other qualities which are generalized. Some connote stability, while others suggest movement, agitation, or calmness. Lines can also create optical illusions. The sensitive designer will discover these characteristics and take advantage of their qualities.

A line meeting itself encloses an area which is called a *shape*. A flat silhouette that is either solid or partially filled is also a shape, and it can be either representational or abstract. Using the techniques of fabric decoration, the designer is free to apply a great diversity of shapes to the cloth surface. Some shapes are more readily achieved with one technique than with another. Thus the individual must become familiar with the unique qualities of each medium in order to express his ideas most successfully.

Color is the most complex of the elements of design, and much has been written about it. A number of color systems or theories have been developed, beginning with that of Sir Isaac Newton in the seventeenth century. Systems currently in use are the Ives, Munsell, Otswald, and Prang. All of these have certain terminology in common, while they differ in complexity and means of classification. It is our intention here to give the information necessary for the craftsman to conduct investigations of his own to gain an understanding of the use of color in fabric decoration.

"Lines," designed by Alexander Girard for Herman Miller Textiles, screen print on cotton. A simple use of lines creates a rhythm through repetition.

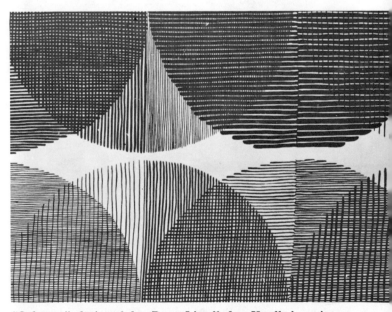

"Spheres," designed by Ross Littell for Knoll Associates Inc., screen print, pigment on fiber glass. Lines of several weights are used to create complex shapes.

41

Block print, resist on cotton, India, 20th century. Dots are used to create lines, and some of the dot-lines enclose shapes.

"Feathers," designed by Alexander Girard for Herman Miller Textiles, screen print on cotton and polyester. Shapes creating more shapes by overprinting are used in simple repetition to achieve a flowing pattern.

"Quatrefoil," designed by Alexander Girard for Herman Miller Textiles, screen print on cotton. Surface pattern is achieved by repetition of a basic shape in six colors.

The terms used to describe the characteristics of color are hue, value, and intensity (chroma). Hue refers to the basic or pure color. The number of hues in the systems listed above varies from twelve to twenty-four. For purposes of clarity, we shall utilize the Prang system, which is based on three primary hues (yellow, red, and blue), three secondary hues, and six intermediate hues. The secondary hues (orange, violet, and green) are formed by combining each of the primaries with one of the other two. These six hues are placed equidistantly around a circle to form a color wheel. Combining each of the six hues with its neighbor creates the six intermediates (yellow-orange, red-orange, red-violet, blue-violet, blue-green, and yellow-green). The wheel is now complete with twelve basic hues.

Value refers to the lightness or darkness of a color and is designated in terms of the amount of white or black that has been added to it. If white is added to a hue, the resulting color is called a tint and is higher in value than the original hue. If black is added to a hue, the resulting color is called a shade and is lower in value than the original hue. When gray is added to a hue, a tone is created.

It should be noted that when working with dyes, tints or higher values are achieved by extending or weakening the concentration of the color with special extender or water, while when working with pigments, white or an extender is added.

Intensity (chroma) refers to the saturation of a hue in any color. To lower the intensity of a hue, its complement, the color directly across from it on the color wheel, is added. This will tend to gray or neutralize the hue. Intensity is also decreased by any change in value.

The use of color in fabric decoration requires an understanding of the terms defined above and an ability to use the properties which colors possess. Whether the craftsman is using pigments or dyes, the principles are the same (except as indicated above in the section on value). There is obviously wide latitude in mixing colors prior to printing, but unique to fabric decoration is the potential for creating additional colors by means of overprinting. This technique of laying one transparent color over another to create a third on the fabric is readily accomplished with dyes and is possible with pigments if the color has been extended to make it transparent.

Texture involves an interrelationship between the visual and tactile senses. In fabric decoration the craftsman is dealing with a fabric surface which may have strong textural qualities itself. In addition, a visual texture can be added in a variety of ways through the effective contrast of spacing and size of shapes and lines. Each decorating technique will contribute textural effects, since the shapes and lines which make up the texture are the result of

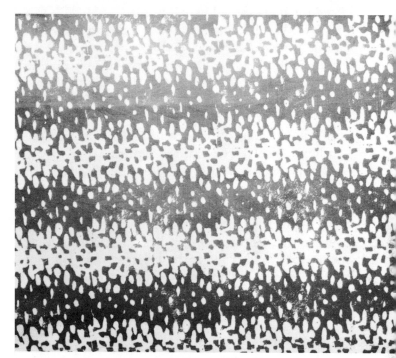

Linoleum-block print. Textured surface is used to create stripes of light and dark.

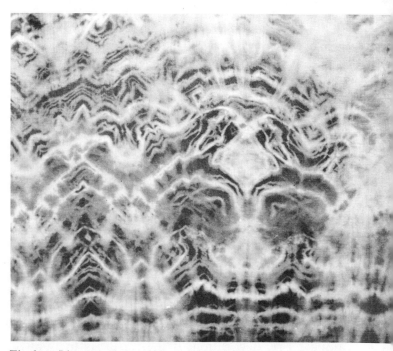

Tie-dye. Lines and irregular shapes result in a broken, textured surface.

43

the tools and materials of that particular technique.

Space is illusionary on a two-dimensional surface. It is created by the knowledgeable use of individual elements or a combination of them. The individual characteristics of each of the elements contrasting with the others will suggest spatial relationships. Thus, thick lines may seem to advance and thin lines recede if hue and value are judiciously used to emphasize the illusion. Contrasts of the individual characteristics of shape, texture, and color, too, all can contribute to the illusion of movement in space. It should be noted, however, that the feeling of space may be affected by the use to which the fabric is put. If it is draped, new spatial relationships may result as original ones become altered by light and shadow and distortion of the pattern.

The elements of design described above—line, shape, color, texture, and space—are interrelated in application on the basis of certain principles of design. Again it should be made clear that any terms used in describing approaches to design are not meant to provide rigid formulas or perfect solutions to any problem. They can be useful in analysis of decorated fabrics and in helping the craftsman to achieve more successful results.

Principles of Design

Rhythm is achieved through some form of repetition that creates a feeling of movement or flow on a fabric surface. There are specific ways in which rhythm can be achieved. One is by continuous repetition of a single element or a set combination of them, resulting in an allover pattern. Another is by a progressive change in the unit as it is repeated. This change can be in size, shape, texture, or color.

The principle of rhythm lies at the core of design for fabric decoration because repetition of a motif is inherent in a number of techniques. The repeated pattern which creates a flow over the entire surface, whether it is flat, draped, or covering a three-dimensional form, is of primary concern. It is extremely important that the craftsman have an understanding of the importance of rhythm in design for fabric surfaces. In the succeeding chapters those who are unfamiliar with this principle will have the opportunity to experiment with its application and gain understanding through direct involvement.

While rhythm is a primary concern in the design of fabric surfaces, there are other principles that are useful in developing the repeat, the basic unit of much fabric decoration. If the repeat is thought of as a composed unit which relates to itself, these

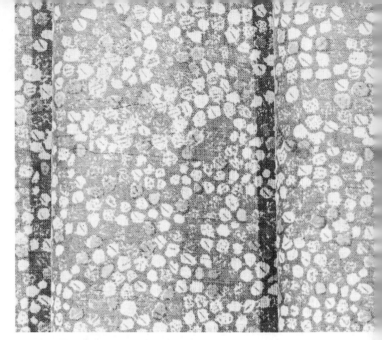

"Pebbles," by Ruth Adler Schnee, screen print on linen. Small irregular shapes contrasting with a dark ground give a feeling of texture.

"Primavera," designed by Don Wight for Jack Lenor Larsen Inc., detail of a screen print on cotton velvet. Contrasting values are positioned to give a feeling of space.

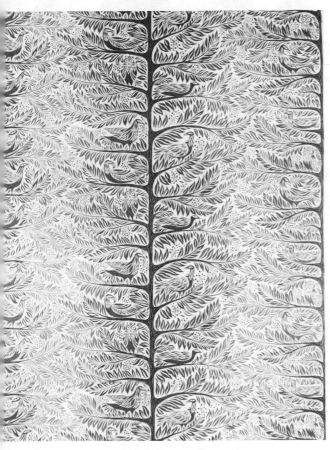

Block print, resist on cotton, India, 12th–14th century. Rhythm is created by repetition of a single unit and use of space that is equal to shape. (The Metropolitan Museum of Art, Gift of V. Everit Macy, 1930)

"Haven," by Elenhank Designers Inc., screen print. A feeling of space is created by combining strong dark linear shapes with light broken areas.

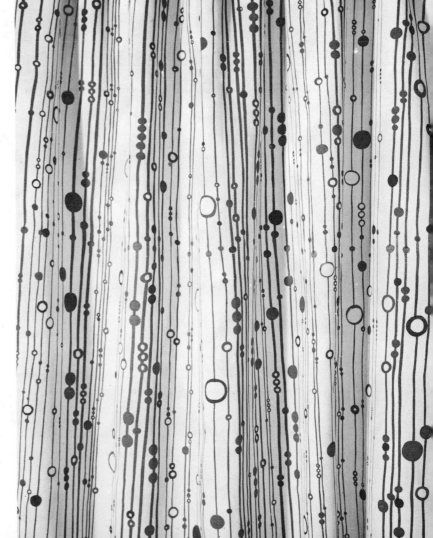

"Strings and Things," by Ruth Adler Schnee, two-color screen print on cotton. Rhythm is created by repetition of a basic shape—the circle—that changes in size, value, and spacing.

"Facets," designed by Jason Harvey for Knoll Associates Inc., screen print on fiber glass. This design illustrates symmetrical balance.

Fragment of a resist print on cotton, India, 14th-15th century. Found in Fostat, Egypt. The curvilinear lines create asymmetrical balance. (Courtesy of The Cooper Union Museum)

other guiding factors can be helpful. However, they are useful only if they do not destroy or adversely affect the rhythm of the unit repeated.

Balance is that principle which implies stability. The stability may be real because it is due to an equal arrangement of elements, or it may be illusionary. Symmetry and asymmetry are two qualities that can give balance to a design. Symmetry can be classified as axial when the balance is created along a line or axis by a mirrored image, and as radial when the balanced parts radiate from a central point. A cross is an example of the first type, while a star or sunburst illustrates the second. Asymmetrical balance can be achieved in a variety of ways through imaginative manipulation of the elements of design. The size and number of shapes and their relation to a central point can create a feeling of balance, as can the effective placement of color on a fabric surface.

Emphasis is that aspect of design which creates a focal point or center of interest and brings attention to a specific area. Emphasis, like balance, can be achieved through the well planned use of the elements of design. It can result from lines that direct attention or from the placement of shapes. Color can be an effective tool for creating emphasis. By variation or contrast in hue, value, or intensity, a center of interest can be established. Texture and a greater or lesser degree of detail can have similar results.

The designer should consider the *compatibility* of the various qualities of the basic unit in order to achieve a harmonious result. Flowing brushstrokes are not readily combined with hard-edged, precise geometric shapes in a single repeat. This does not mean that a variety of shapes, lines, or textures cannot be combined in a unit. It does mean that careful thought and planning are required if the allover rhythm of the surface is not to be destroyed by discordant components.

"Windbreak," by Elenhank Designers Inc., screen print. Emphasis is achieved by a contrast of value.

Painted cotton, Peru, ca. 1100-1400. Emphasis is achieved by variation in shape and spacing. (The Textile Museum, Washington, D.C.)

When the elements of design have been combined in such a way that the fabric surface has a satisfying sense of rhythm, the design can be said to possess *unity*. Any final analysis of a particular fabric design, however, must be reserved until the fabric is put to some use. Are the relationships satisfying when it is made into a garment, gathered into drapery folds, covering a wall, chair, or sofa? The answer to these questions will determine whether the specific design exhibits unity.

It should be emphasized that no section of this book will provide instant design inspiration for the craftsman. The survey of historical and contemporary fabric decoration has been included to provide those interested with a background in the evolution of styles and techniques. The challenge, then, is to use techniques and designs which are a reflection of today's world and not to rely on past cultures for easy and quick solutions.

Coupled with a knowledge of the history of fabric decoration, therefore, should be an acute awareness of our present environment, both natural and man-made. We gain knowledge of our environment through meaningful perceptual experiences. In fabric design, the visual and tactile experiences are of greatest importance. If we are interested in expanding the reserve upon which creative design is built, these experiences cannot be left to chance. Perception is a dynamic process in which sensation is related to the individual's accumulated experiences. Increased sensitivity to the environment can lead to a new awareness, and this awareness can have direct results in design for a fabric surface. A walk through a wood in spring may suggest an arrangement of lines, a combination of shapes, or subtle variations in color that, when related to past experiences, can result in sketches, refinements, and, eventually, a fabric print.

Each person is unique in his range and combination of experiences, and since design is related to these experiences, the designs each craftsman creates should also possess a uniqueness which is an expression of the individual. A design for fabric is the result of a unique idea combined with a process that utilizes certain materials. The idea is of first importance, because it brings a sense of unity to all the elements of the design.

3. Planning a Design

The vocabulary of design outlined in the preceding chapter provides a groundwork that will give meaning to experiences with materials and processes. There is no substitute for the understanding gained by direct involvement with the techniques of decorating fabrics.

There are, of course, many ways to approach the design of a fabric surface. One that is emphasized throughout this book is based on an understanding of the potentials of each technique. In order to realize what the potentials are, the craftsman is encouraged to experiment freely with the tools, materials, and processes of each technique to get the feel of its unique qualities. This experimentation may lead to the idea for a specific design or suggest the way in which an existing idea can be realized. The free exploration of the potentials of a technique is not meant to result in any kind of finished design. It should suggest ways of ornamenting a fabric surface with a design and a process that are compatible.

In addition, the craftsman should explore tools, materials, and processes of graphic design that may or may not be directly related to a specific decorating technique. The suggestions for experimentation which follow are intended to give the craftsman a variety of experiences in design. These experiments will result in arrangements of design elements that may be utilized in design for fabrics and that will be a personal expression of the craftsman.

These arrangements, or basic units, may be put into a repeated pattern, and methods for planning a repeat are described below. The use of color, another important consideration in planning a design, is discussed in the final section of the chapter.

Design Experiments

Paper can be manipulated in a number of ways to gain experience with line, shape, and space. It is recommended that color not be a primary concern in the experiments outlined in this section.
(1) Cut a number of identical shapes from folded black paper and arrange them on a grid in a variety of repeated patterns. Glue down the patterns which use the shapes in repetition effectively. Repeat the experiment with strips of black paper which vary in length and width.

(2) Divide a space in either a symmetrical or an asymmetrical way by cutting a rectangle of black paper into pieces. Arrange them on a piece of white paper in the following ways: (a) discard some pieces and use space as an element; (b) use all the pieces and space them equally; (c) use all the pieces and space them unequally. Glue down the effective patterns.

(3) Fold a piece of black paper in halves, quarters, or eighths and cut out a series of shapes. Note the symmetry created both in the cut-out shapes and the remaining skeleton as a result of the folding. Place the skeleton on a piece of white paper and glue it down. On another piece arrange the cut-out shapes in a symmetrical pattern, trying variations in spacing. When a satisfactory pattern is achieved, glue the pieces in place.

(4) Repeat the exercises suggested above with torn paper and study the characteristics resulting from the use of this particular process in contrast to those achieved with cut paper.

(5) Fold or pleat rice paper horizontally, vertically, or diagonally and dip the edges in waterproof ink. Analyze the relationship between the method of folding and the resulting patterns.

(6) Select a small object with a flat side that will print a shape. Corks, spools, blocks of wood, or household objects of plastic can be used. Use tempera, designer's colors, or printer's ink to print the shape in many possible arrangements. Try numerous variations, including patterns of stripes or spots or allover effects.

(7) Use brushes, pens, and sticks with a liquid medium to make lines and shapes. Study the special qualities that result from using each particular tool on various surfaces.

(8) Dip sponges, crumpled paper, plastic, or fabric in liquid media such as paint or ink and experiment with the novel textural effects they give when printed.

(9) Manipulate liquid media by spraying, dribbling, and pouring and study the design potentials of these processes.

Symmetrical design made with folded and cut paper in repeat.

Rice paper folded and dipped in ink.

Design made with torn tissue paper.

Screen print, torn paper used for the stencil.

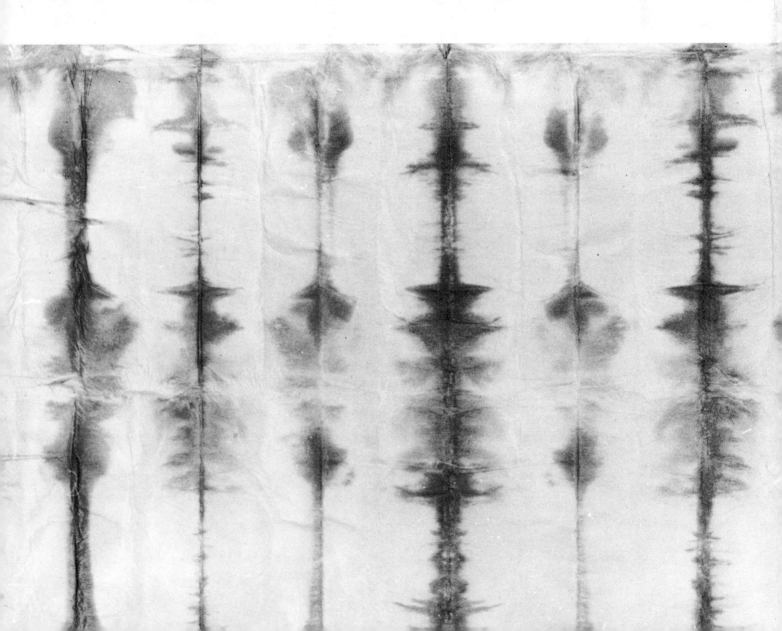

A variety of arrangements made by stamping a simple shape on paper.

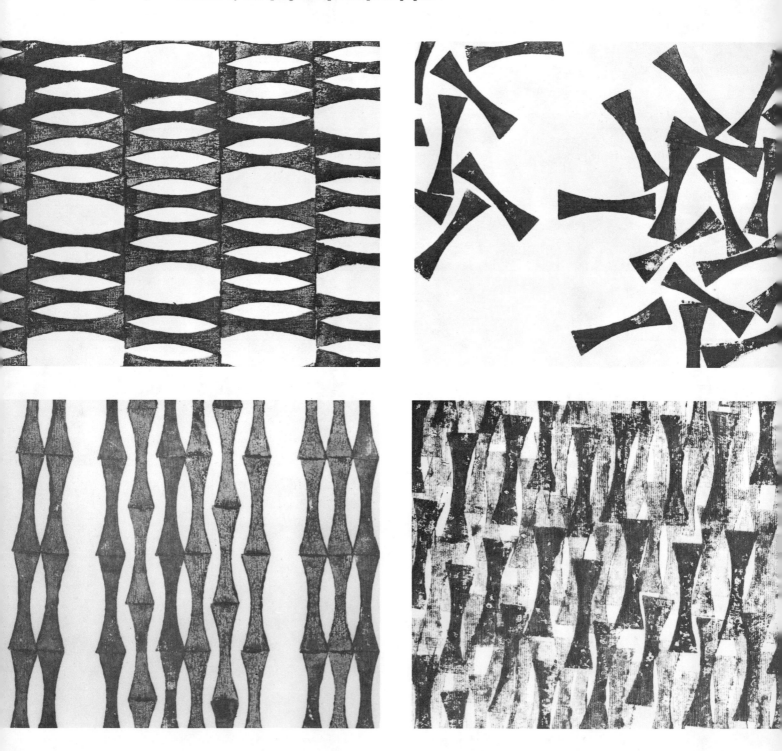

More variations in the arrangement of a shape stamped on paper.

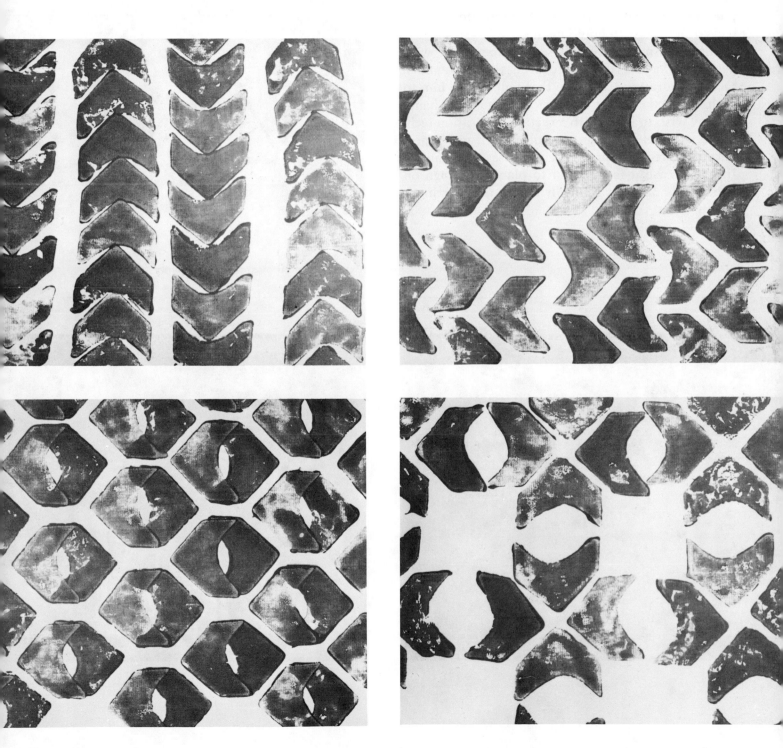

(10) Experiment with traditional drawing techniques using pencil, charcoal, crayon, and pastel. Note the graphic effects created by using these media on different materials: for example, the texture achieved with crayon on a rough surface.

Many of the experiments described above can be duplicated in specific fabric decoration techniques, while others can be adapted to achieve similar results. Design techniques involving cutting can be realized in cut-film screen printing; brushwork can be utilized in screen printing or direct methods. The photographic screen process can duplicate most effects produced with liquid media.

The craftsman may choose to experiment with design media and, after discovering their potentials, seek a decoration technique that will enable him to realize a certain effect on fabric. On the other hand, he may wish to work with a certain decoration technique and seek a design medium which will reproduce the effects on paper for purposes of planning. In either case it is essential to plan the design on paper and analyze it critically before transferring it to fabric.

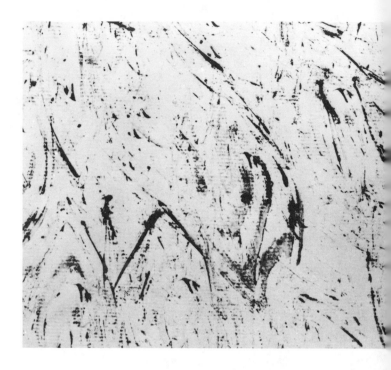

Textures created by stamping on paper.

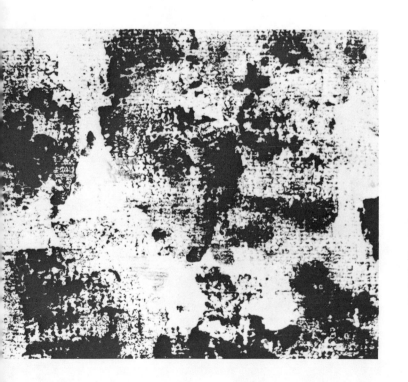

Screen print on fold-and-dye ground. The symmetrical cut-paper design was made with a cut-film stencil.

Direct painting with dyes. Brushstroke and wet-on-wet effects are achieved through this direct approach.

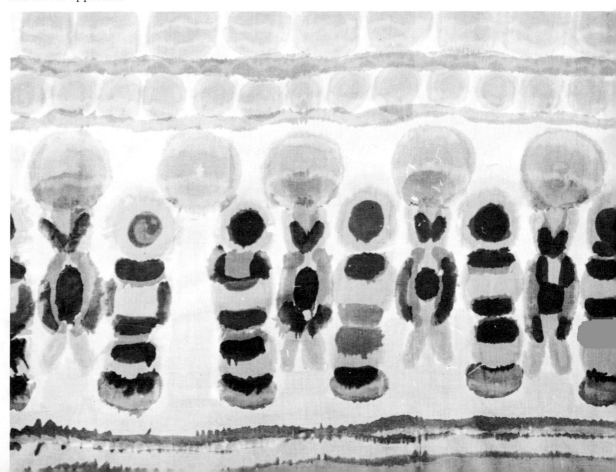

Repeats

The repeat is the basic unit of design in the decoration of fabric by printing techniques, and it may also be desirable with direct methods, resists, and tie-dye. Once the basic unit has been established, it must be put into repeat. Repetition of the basic unit should create a rhythmic flow over the whole fabric.

The basic unit may repeat in a number of ways, as illustrated. These examples should be considered as guidelines; the craftsman may arrive at his own variations depending on the technique used and the nature of the basic unit.

There are a number of decisions that must be made concerning the basic unit before it can be put into repeat. One of these is its size, which is influenced by several factors. The technique used determines the maximum size of a single unit. The width of the cloth to be decorated also affects the size of the repeat. Standard widths vary from 36 to 54 inches, and the repeat should be adapted to the fabric selected.

The method of joining one basic unit with the next should also be considered early in repeat planning. There are three ways in which this can be accomplished. In a butt joint the units meet each other along a straight line. This can be used when the unit consists of a series of shapes or lines arranged in rows. In the dovetail joint a portion of one unit fits into a part of the next, without touching it. The overlapping joint, in which the units overlap, can be used when the effect of a continuous line or shape is required. In using this joint, careful thought must be given to effects created by overprinting.

There is an optical device that is helpful in determining whether a design will be satisfactory in repeat before the final adjustments of the unit are made on paper. It requires two mirrors, each big enough to reflect the basic unit. They are placed at right angles to each other, perpendicular to and at one corner of the unit. So placed, the mirrors will reflect the unit in repetition, giving the illusion of a continuous design.

Tracing paper in large sheets or in rolls provides a way to put a unit into repeat. This paper should be used freely to make the first rough layouts and the adjustments of the final repeat. A piece of tracing paper large enough to accommodate at least four repeats is placed over the unit so that the unit occupies one quarter of the paper. Assuming that the internal arrangement of the unit is satisfactory, adjustments are made only at the edges. The outer

Types of repeats.

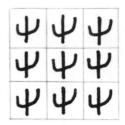

BLOCK

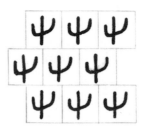

BRICK

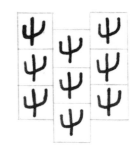

HALF DROPS

DIAMOND

OGEE

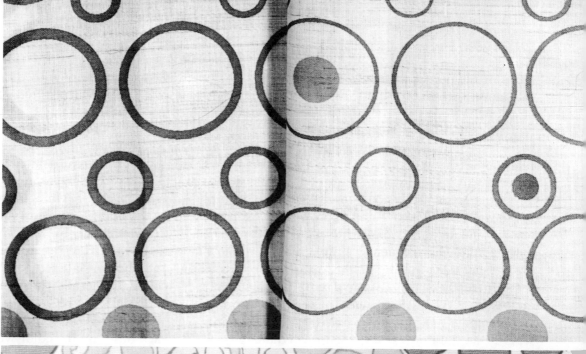

"Cordwood," by Ruth Adler Schnee, screen print. This design repeat can be achieved by using the butt joint along a straight line.

Screen print, by Win Anderson Fabrics Division, Jack Lenor Larsen Inc. This illustrates the kind of design repeat that can be achieved with the dovetail joint.

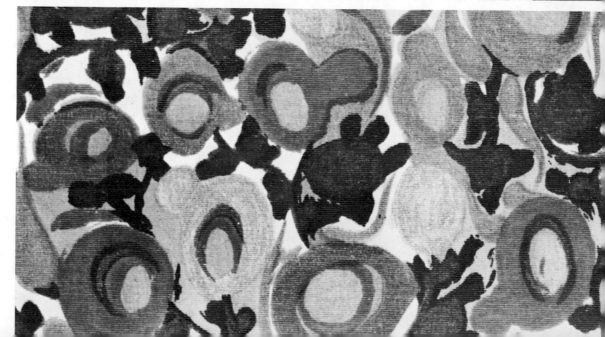

"Windflower," by Jack Lenor Larsen Inc., screen print. The overlapping joint is utilized in this kind of allover, continuous pattern.

edges of the unit are traced with a soft pencil. Now the paper is moved so that the unit is directly above or below the one just traced. The way in which the two units join should be studied, and the spaces occurring between the units should be analyzed in relation to the spaces within the unit. The spaces created will be an integral part of the total design and must be carefully considered. The type of joint to be used should be decided upon, and adjustments are now made to accomplish this.

Butt joints are frequently simple to achieve; however, exact registration in the printing process is imperative. Dovetail joints also require adjustments at this time. With the tracing paper over the unit, the elements are traced in existing positions only where the joining is satisfactory. Where adjustments are necessary, the outlines of elements in new positions are drawn in. For clarity these changes may be drawn in another color pencil. It is advisable to try several variations on tracing paper to ensure the best possible solution. When adjustments for top and bottom have been made, the tracing paper is shifted so that side adjustments can be made in a similar manner. As a final check, the unit should be repeated four times, so that all joinings can be seen, analyzed, and adjusted.

The overlapping joint is frequently the most difficult one to achieve. A color overlapping itself will usually create a darker value, an additional element in the design. The overlap should be considered part of the design and carefully planned or creatively utilized. Its effect may be minimized by careful study of the unit in repeat and selection of the points where overlapping will take place. Narrow shapes, lines, and textures frequently provide the ideal point of joining. The procedure is the same as for dovetail joints, with adjustments made where necessary. A completed drawing that shows the unit joined on all sides will allow the craftsman to determine whether the pattern is unified.

Color

It is possible to plan a design almost to finality without the introduction of color. Each craftsman develops the method of planning best suited to his experience and goals. Some work with color from the beginning, while others prefer to introduce color after a unit is in repeat. However, the craftsman is inevitably faced with decisions about using colors in combination. There are a number of generally agreed upon characteristics which can be used as guides for combining colors. Knowledge of them

may prove helpful to those whose experience with color has been limited. These characteristics fall into two broad categories: those involving related hues and those involving contrasting hues.

Monochromatic colors are derived from one hue; however, a great deal of variety can be achieved by changes in value and intensity. *Analogous* colors are those with one hue in common, such as yellow, green, and blue-green (yellow is the common hue). Colors related by hue are placed in two groups: those related to red are referred to as warm colors, and those related to blue are referred to as cool colors. Generally speaking, warm colors advance and cool ones recede.

Complementary hues are two that lie opposite each other on the color wheel. When they are mixed together, the intensity is lowered, and gray can result. Studies in the physiology of color vision indicate that the same receptors in the retina of the eye are sensitive to complementary colors. Thus, when complementary colors are juxtaposed in certain ways, they tend to reinforce each other. The effect can be one of strong optical vibrations and agitated movement. Judiciously used, for example in points of emphasis, complements can subtly enhance each other. *Split-complement* refers to the combination of a color with the hues on either side of its complement. Orange used with blue-violet and blue-green would be considered a split-complement. A *triad* is a combination that includes any three hues which are equidistant on the color wheel. Orange, green, and violet form a triad. The combination of hues in a triad results in a dominance of either warm or cool colors.

In developing a design it is important to simulate as closely as possible the final effect a dye or pigment will give to a fabric surface. There are several liquid media which resemble dyes when thoughtfully used. Waterproof ink is transparent, and it is readily available for experimenting with color effects. Felt-tipped markers are also readily available and provide another source of transparent color with effects similar to those of dyes. Fabric dyes can also be used for design development on paper by making a small amount of dye into a paste and adding water to achieve the proper intensity of color.

The craftsman may wish to start working with the three primary colors and proceed to more complex relationships. A transparent color can be brushed on paper, allowed to dry, and overlapped with others to experiment with the effect of overprinting. The inks can be lightened by thinning with

Screen print and batik on cotton velvet, by Meda Parker Johnston. Three colors—turquoise, blue-violet, and golden yellow—result in a multicolored fabric through the effective use of overprinting with fiber-reactive dyes.

water and mixed to achieve other colors. The purpose of such exercises is to learn something about the nature of transparent color, and no attempt should be made to create an organized design.

Tempera and designer's colors can be used to simulate the effects created by pigments on fabric. The craftsman may wish to execute some of his work with pigments. Although many effects are possible with them, they have less potential for fabric decoration than dyes.

It is beneficial to execute some sample work with the actual dyes or pigments. To observe the changes in value and intensity that result from overprinting, a series of rectangles or other shapes can be printed in some arrangement, such as a grid, on properly prepared fabric (see Chapter 4 for directions for preparation of the fabric). A good way to experiment is to print a number of sample grids using full-strength and reduced colors in various combinations. Starting with formulas of full-strength

dye or pigment, a series may be printed as follows: full-strength paste, 1 part paste to 1 part extender, 1 part paste to 4 parts extender, and 1 part paste to 10 parts extender. It is important to keep an accurate record of this work and file it for future reference.

When a multicolor design results from printing a separate unit for each color, each color in the rendering can be traced separately to provide a cartoon for preparation of a screen or block. This is called color separation. The separation may be done with tracing paper. Allowances should be made for joining and registration. The original design should have a registration mark (a small cross) that will be matched on each color separation and on the printing device (as described in Chapter 4). Designs with two or more colors are not always the result of this separation, however, but may result from varied placement of a single screen or other printing device.

A basic unit put into repeat on tracing paper.

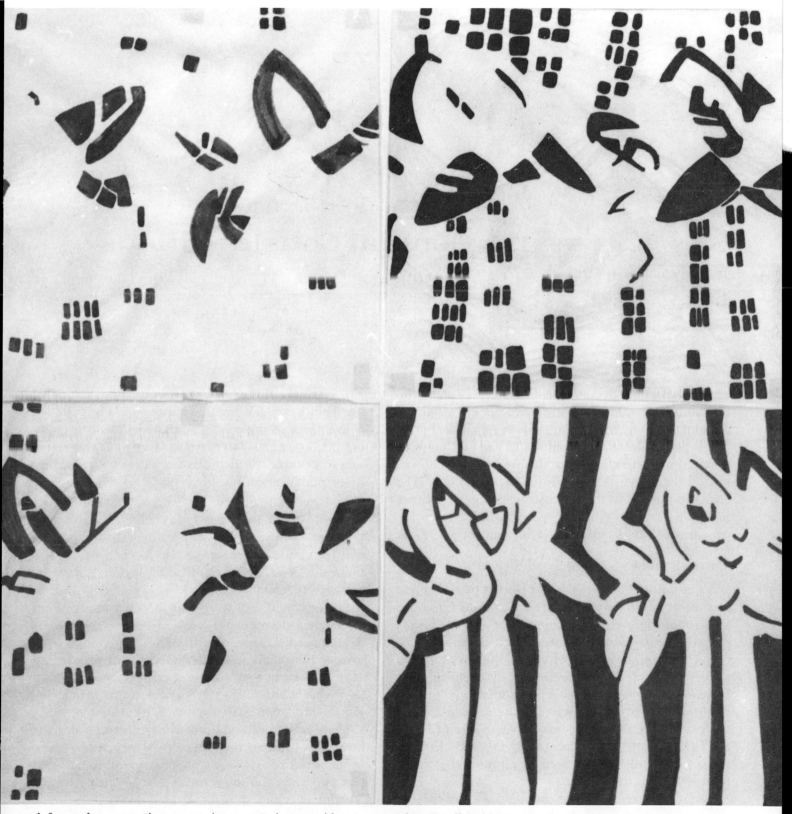

A four-color separation on tracing paper that provides cartoons for stencil-making.

4. General Considerations

The information given in this chapter is basic to the techniques of fabric decoration. It is essential for the craftsman to be familiar with the general characteristics of fabrics and media and the processes of pretreatment, fixation, and finishing in order to obtain satisfactory results with any technique. The craftsman who wishes to use printing techniques must be familiar with the general procedures for preparation of the printing table and registration.

Materials and Equipment

Some equipment is necessary for the planning and execution of all fabric decoration, while there are some materials which are useful and may be acquired gradually by the craftsman. A detailed list of the specific materials required for the various techniques is given at the beginning of each chapter. However, a brief summary of commonly needed equipment is provided here for the convenience of the craftsman. Of course, not all of the items listed are necessary to begin decorating fabrics: they are included to indicate the type of supplies the craftsman will wish to collect.

The work area should be provided with or located near a source of water. Sinks are needed for dyeing and washing, though washtubs can be substituted for them, and a hose with a spray nozzle is an added convenience. A table which can be padded for printing purposes (as described below) will also serve as a work table if it is protected with a cover of muslin or plastic sheeting.

A stove or hot plate, a steam cabinet or improvised substitute (also described below), and a steam iron are necessary appliances for many processes and techniques, and an electric kitchen mixer and fan are useful. A clothesline and plastic clothespins are used for drying fabric.

Scales which will weigh up to 600 grams and an immersion thermometer, such as a candy thermometer, are needed for work with decorating media. Deep pans or tubs of stainless steel, enamel, or plastic and assorted mixing bowls of the same materials are used for dyebaths and mixing dye pastes, as are measuring spoons and a cup with 1-ounce markings.

The usual studio equipment for planning designs includes a drawing board, construction paper, newsprint, sketchpads, tracing paper, and watercolor and rice paper, as well as scissors and a variety of artist's brushes and sponges. Drawing inks, felt-tipped marking pens, watercolors, designer's colors, tem-

A yardstick, ruler, and metal measuring tape are needed, and a good supply of newspaper, absorbent rags, non-absorbent cardboard cut into smooth-edged, small pieces, glass jars with lids, and tin cans should be collected for various purposes. A light table or box is required for preparing photographic stencils in screen printing, and it is a convenience for transferring designs onto fabric (a dressmaker's carbon and tracing wheel may also be used for this purpose). A light table can be improvised by placing a piece of plate glass over upright supports and clamping a light underneath.

Finally, a supply of a kitchen cleanser of the abrasive type, household bleach, color remover, waterproof glue, mineral spirits, turpentine, spar varnish and solvent, and shellac and solvent should be kept on hand in the studio.

Fabrics

The following section on Media explains in detail the possible combinations of fabrics and decorating media. In general, the most successful fabric decoration using dyestuffs, with the materials and equipment available to the average craftsman, will be achieved on the natural fibers: cotton, linen, silk, and wool. Viscose rayon is the one man-made fiber that is especially recommended. (Methods for identifying the various types of fibers are given in Chapter X.) Cotton and linen which have been mercerized have greater affinity for dyes because of the chemicals used in the mercerizing process. A wider range of fabrics can be utilized when pigments are the media used for decoration. These media can be applied to the man-made fibers and blends as well as to all the natural ones. Very inexpensive fabrics are good for experimenting with repeats and design ideas, but they give unsatisfactory results when decorated with some dyes.

Fabrics to be decorated can be sheer or closely woven, and their surface textured or plain. These individual characteristics may inspire designs, or a fabric with certain characteristics may be chosen because it is appropriate for the spirit of a preconceived design. The choice of weight and texture is also influenced by the final use of the fabric, whether for upholstery, drapery, pillows, wall hangings, apparel, etc.

be familiar with the types of media that can be used in the techniques of fabric decoration and with their characteristics, which will influence the choice of an appropriate medium, and this information is summarized here.

The various techniques of fabric decoration require various methods of color application. In block printing, screen printing, and painting, color is applied in pastes. Resist techniques require cold baths of color, and tie-dyeing can be done in either hot or cold baths. The craftsman may choose either dyes or pigments to make pastes, while only dyes can be used for color baths.

Safety in Surface Design

Many of the materials used in surface-design techniques are potentially dangerous to health and safety if not used with intelligence and care. These materials include dyes and chemical assistants which are considered industrial chemicals, solvents, waxes, and other substances that are important to the variety of processes covered in subsequent chapters.

Recent concern with health hazards, coupled with increased observation and research, has resulted in an additional amount of information available to the surface design artist. Harmful materials are divided into two groups: *toxic* materials that can cause serious damage to the body upon contact or can subsequently lead to serious injury or disease and *hazardous* materials that are capable of causing damage under certain conditions of use or exposure.

The primary areas of the body that are susceptible to chemical stress are the lungs, kidneys, liver, and skin. The lungs and skin are most susceptible to dyes, chemicals, and other materials used in surface design and these are of fundamental concern. Hypersensitivity or allergy can lead to complications, and the artist must be aware of these possibilities. Safe working practices can maintain good health and the enjoyment of working in surface design.

Some groups of people are more susceptible to negative effects of contact with hazardous materials, and special care should be exercised. These include infants and small children, aged persons or those with heart and lung conditions, asthmatics, smokers, persons with kidney or liver diseases, allergic persons, and pregnant women. Anyone in these categories should consult a physician before beginning extensive work in surface design.

Definition and Classification of Dyes

A dye may be defined as a colored substance, usually applied in an aqueous solution, that may be attached to a material with some degree of permanence. Pigments, on the other hand, are not dissolved in application processes but remain solid particles that are attached to fibers with resin binders.

Dyes contain two chemical features: chromophores, which enable them to appear a particular color, and auxochromes, which aid in holding the dye within the fiber. Chromophores are unsaturated groups of atoms which may be considered as areas of electron density that allow light of specific wavelengths to be absorbed (i.e., violet) by the molecule, creating the sensation of a specific color (i.e., yellow-green). Auxochromes in the dye interact with the fiber molecule to form a temporary or permanent bond. This ability of the auxochromes to aid in attaching the dye to the fiber is directly related to the fastness of a particular dye on a particular fiber. This attachment can be either physical or chemical. A description of the various dyes classified by application will include a discussion of the means by which the dye is held in the fiber.

Dyes can be classified in a variety of ways, including source (vegetable, animal, mineral, synthetic), molecular structure (nitro, azo, stilbene, etc.), or application (acid, basic, direct, disperse, reactive, vat). The latter classification is the one in most common use in surface design and will be used throughout this text.

The greatest danger from dyes seems to be from those of the benzidine type, which are components of various dyes used to achieve specific colors on certain fibers. Benzidine has been classified as a human carcinogen by the Occupational Safety and Health Administration. Information available indicates that benzidine-type components are used in many direct dyes and to some degree in disperse and napthol dyes. There may be others that contain these components. When in doubt question the supplier or manufacturer to ascertain whether there are any benzidine-type components in a specific dye.

ACID DYES

These dyes are so named because of the presence in the dye molecule of a sulfonic-acid-salt chemical group. The attraction between dye and fiber in this class is an electrostatic one between the acid part of the dye and the basic amino groups in the fiber. These dyes are available in a wide range of brilliant colors and are used on wool, silk, and nylon. There are two types of acid dyes: *leveling*, which have smaller molecules, give a uniform color, but require strong acids and have poor wetfastness; *milling* dyes have larger molecules and can be applied from weak acid baths. The latter type are recommended for the studio surface designer. Acid dyes are a component in most household and some craft dyes.

These dyes may have the least potential for harmful effects of all classes. The majority of food colorings are from the acid group because they are highly ionized and not readily absorbed into the body; however, some of these dyes have been indicated as cancer-causing when ingested. Chemical burns are a possibility. Caution is required in the use of the acid (acetic) required in most baths with the milling type.

BASIC DYES

The origins of the synthetic-dye industry are found in the discovery of *mauveine*, a basic dye derived from coal tar, by W. H. Perkin in 1856. This class of dye is called basic or cationic because of the positive charge of the primary dye chromophore. The dyes have a natural affinity for wool and silk but can be used on cellulosic fibers that have been premodanted with tannic acid. Basic dyes have brilliance of color, including the "day-glow" colors, but in general have poor fastness to light. These dyes are often components of household and craft dyes, along with acid and direct.

Like acid dyes, basic dyes are highly ionized and are thus less likely to be absorbed by the body. The same precautions should be exercised as for acid dyes.

DIRECT DYES

Direct dyes, first developed by Böttinger in 1884, were the first available that did not require a complicated application procedure and were the predecessors of the first household dyes. Congo Red was the first of these dyes and is still in extensive use today. The dye in this class is held to the fiber molecule by a hydrogen-bonding action that is mechanical rather than chemical. This bond is not as strong as in other dyes and is more easily disrupted. Although a wide range of colors is available, there is a general lack of brilliance and fastness to light and washing. These dyes are used primarily on cellulosic fibers. Direct dyes are a basic ingredient in many household and craft dyes, along with acid and basic. "The direct dye component is always present for cotton fabrics."[*]

Benzidine-type components are a basic ingredient in many direct dyes. The dangers of these benzidine-type components as carcinogens has been covered in

*Jenkins, C. L., "Textile Dyes Are Potential Hazards." *Journal of Environmental Health*, March/April. 40:256, 1978.

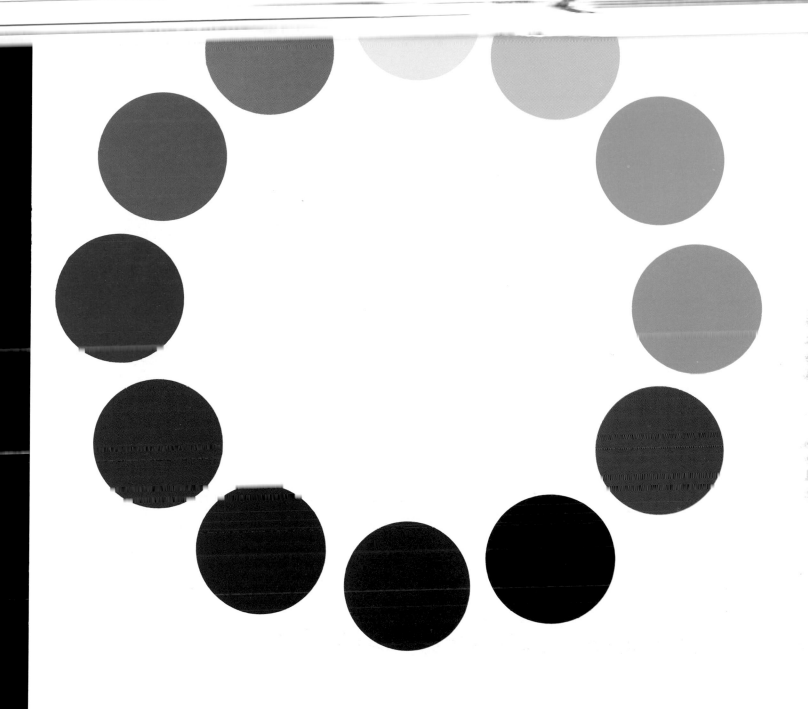

The Prang 12-hue color wheel. Reading clockwise from the top, the hues are: yellow, yellow-green, green, blue-green, blue, blue-violet, violet, red-violet, red, red-orange, orange, and yellow-orange.

Fold-and-dye with fiber-reactive dyes, by Ronald Goodman.

Tie-dye on linen, by Meda Parker Johnston.

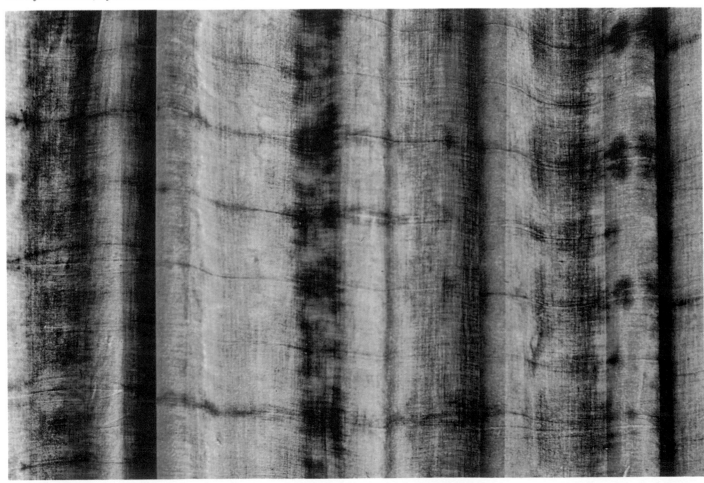

Paste resist decoration on silk, Japan, 20th century.

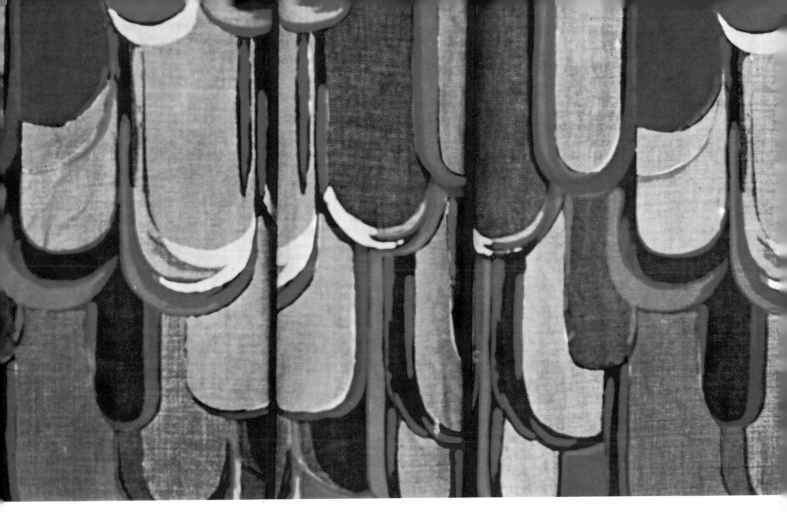

Screen print on linen, by Meda Parker Johnston.

turer of household dye, Rit, has reformulated its dyes so as not to contain benzidine-type dyes.* Other potential problems are: powder is caustic, allergic reactions, lung irritation.

DISPERSE DYES

This class of dyes was developed in 1972 by Green and Saunders in England for dyeing cellulose acetate. The problem with this fiber and some other synthetics is that it is hydrophobic (nonabsorptive of water) and dyes in a water solution cannot penetrate the fiber. The dye is *dispersed* in a water bath, moves into the fiber, and dissolves there because it is chemically more like the fiber than the water. These dyes are used on acetate, polyester, acrylic, and nylon.

Disperse dyes can be used in a bath with the aid of a carrier, which helps swell the fiber and allow the dye to penetrate and dissolve. Disperse dyes can also be printed on polyester and other synthetic fabrics by the transfer process. The dyes are applied first to paper by a variety of means; the dye-covered paper and fabric are put into contact with heat; and the dye is transferred by the sublimation process (dye vaporizes and recondenses in the fiber of the fabric). There is a range of colors available, and fastness to light and washing is good.

"As a class, only disperse dyes have caused widespread dermatitis from the finished product."* This should be a concern to surface designers who are dyeing with disperse dyes, especially clothing; contact with the dye in powder or solution can cause skin irritations, possibly cancer with some. Special caution should be exercised in the use of carriers needed with disperse dyes in a bath. Some carriers give off strong fumes that can cause headaches and nausea. All carriers should be used in a well-ventilated room.

REACTIVE DYES

The first application of reactive dyes to cotton was achieved by Rattee and Stephen of Imperial Chemical Industries in 1956. The reaction here between the dye and fiber molecules is a covalent bond in which there is a permanent sharing of electrons. This results in greatly increased fastness to washing and allows the use of dyes with comparatively simple structures and high diffusion rates with improved brightness in a wide range of colors. Reactive dyes can be applied to cellulosic fibers as well as wool and silk.

them in the fiber. These dyes are widely used by surface designers and are packaged under a variety of trade names.

Reactive dyes are very reactive chemicals that are capable of reacting with the body's tissues as well as with fibers. The respiratory system is especially sensitive to these dyes, and allergic reactions or asthma may result from breathing dye powder.

Special caution is needed in handling reactive dyes since they are best stored in the powder form and mixed as needed. Unlike other dyes, the reactives are not recommended to be stored in stock solutions because they react with the water in solution and weaken in strength. I.C.I. treats its Procion dyes to minimize the formation of dust.

VAT DYES

Indigo is one of the oldest vat dyes known, used perhaps as early as 2000 B.C. Other natural dyes, including the Imperial Purple of ancient Rome, are of this type. Heumann developed a synthetic indigo in 1897, and this lead to further developments in the field. The first step in preparing vat dyes is reduction with sodium hydroxide or sodium hydrosulfite to a colorless soluble compound. The fabric is saturated with the colorless dye and then allowed to oxidize to the colored insoluble state within the fiber. All vat dyes are suitable for cellulosic fibers and some can be used on wool. They are very fast to washing but are not extensive in color range. Prepared vat dyes are available for studio use in a paste form that oxidizes to the insoluble state upon exposure to sunlight or heat.

Some vat dyes in the powdered form are caustic compared with other dyes and can cause irritation to the respiratory system. Other vat dyes, including indigo, require the use of sodium hydroxide, which is extremely corrosive to all tissue.

PIGMENTS

Pigments are generally brilliant in color and have relatively good fastness to light and washing. They can be easily applied to most fibers, except wool, by printing and some direct methods. The range of colors available is more limited than that of dyes. Most are sold as pastes that require little preparation prior to use. Each manufacturer supplies specific information on fastness and directions for use which the craftsman should follow for reliable results. Textile pigments may be classified according

*Craft Horizons, August 1976, p. 68.
*Jenkins, C. L., Journal of Environmental Health, March/April 1978.

or suspended.

Emulsion pigments are the most widely used group and are available from a number of manufacturers. Most are based on oil or synthetic resin and water which, with some brands, is used as thinner and solvent for clean-up.

Synthetic-base pigments use synthetic oil or resin as a binder and are thinned and cleaned up with solvents such as mineral spirits.

Oil-based pigments employ a natural oil as a binder. Printer's inks can be used satisfactorily for block printing and some direct methods, but are not suitable for screen printing.

Pigments are easy to apply and fix without special equipment. They can be used for both opaque or transparent color, in contrast to dyes, which are always transparent. However, the disadvantages of using pigments are that they obscure the natural qualities of the fiber and do not seem a part of the fabric because they lie on the surface. Fabrics decorated with pigments also are slightly stiff of hand.

It is sometimes desirable to achieve a light-colored design on a dark ground. Pigment pastes can be used to print a light color on a dark ground if they are sufficiently opaque. With dyestuffs there are two general methods for obtaining this effect: by discharging existing color and by resisting color. The discharge method can be used with any of the decorating techniques by starting with a colored fabric and applying a bleaching substance to remove the color in the design areas. In the resist method, design areas of a light ground are reserved or protected with some substance which will resist dark color applied over it. (This process is the basis of batik and related techniques of decoration, and tie-dyeing also utilizes a form of resist.)

What to Do

STUDIO SPACE

A work space should be selected that is separate from the living area. One should not work in the kitchen. Contact with the materials used in surface design should be avoided by other persons, especially small children. Proper ventilation is essential when working with dye powders, batik wax, or processes that result in the production of fumes. A local exhaust system that traps contaminated air near its source by means of a hood and ducts is ideal.

Special equipment noted earlier in this chapter and in subsequent chapters should be used for surface-design activities exclusively. No kitchen equipment should be used in the studio.

HOUSEKEEPING and STORAGE

A well-arranged studio should be designed for easy cleaning and include adequate storage. Work surfaces should be covered with paper that can be removed daily. Any spills of dye powder or solution, chemicals, or assistants should be wiped up immediately. Vacuuming and wet mopping of floors are preferable to sweeping, as the latter tends to send any dye powder into the air.

PERSONAL HYGIENE

Personal habits practiced in the studio can reduce health hazards. NO eating or smoking should be done in the studio area where contamination is possible. Gloves and protective clothing should be worn when working with dyes or chemicals, and this clothing should be changed, left in the studio, and washed frequently. Hands should be washed when leaving the studio area.

KNOW YOUR MATERIALS

You should always know what you are using and the proper precautions necessary. Read all manufacturers' and suppliers' instructions and labels very carefully. If you are not satisfied with the information available, ask for more from the supplier. Seek less toxic or nontoxic alternatives to materials you know are hazardous and exercise care in the use of all dyes, chemicals, and related materials.

HANDLING DYE POWDERS

All dye powders are composed of small particles that can easily become airborne and create a potential hazard. These powders should always be kept in sealed containers to prevent unnecessary escape into the air. Proper ventilation is essential and can be accomplished by a variety of means: removal of air by means of a fan in a wall or window; trapping contaminated air near its source by means of a hood and ducts; adding air through doors, windows, fans, etc.; bringing in clean air to replace that removed by exhaust fans. The best system for extensive use of dye powders and/or wax fumes is the local exhaust system that traps contaminated air by means of a hood and ducts.

When handling dye powders gloves and protective clothing should be worn. There is a wide variety of should be worn when working with dye powders. Air-purifying respirators have interchangeable filters designed to filter dusts and chemicals of all types. There are several brands available with sources listed in the Suppliers' list. Protective goggles should be worn if eye irritation is a problem.

Long-handled stainless steel spoons (iced tea) are convenient for handling dye powders and are recommended. When mixing dyes it is recommended that the powder be pasted with water immediately after measuring. A stock solution of dye powder and water is a safer, more convenient, and more accurate way of handling the dye. It is discussed in detail in Chapter 11. Reactive dyes do not lend themselves to prolonged storage in stock solutions as the dye reacts with the water in the absence of fiber and effectiveness is diminished and color unreliable after a period of storage.

Dye Solutions

Dyes in solutions avoid the hazards of inhaled dust but pose other problems. Gloves and protective clothing should be worn to avoid direct contact with the skin. If unavoidable contact is made between dye in solution and the hands or other parts of the body, one should wash with soap and plenty of water. Special care should be exercised when working with concentrated or short dye baths as in fold-and-dye, batik, and direct application. All spills should be wiped up immediately. Care should be taken when using solutions in a spray bottle, spray can, or airbrush. Proper ventilation should be available and mask or respirator used to prevent inhalation of dye in the form of a fine mist.

Chemical Assistants

Care should be exercised in the use of chemicals required with the various dyes, discharges, and other processes. The chart in Chapter 11 lists the assistants in common use and any potential hazards.

Wax

Melted waxes used in batik pose fire and respiratory hazards. Wax should always be melted in a device that allows for temperature control. This is discussed in detail in Chapter 8. Proper temperature control greatly reduces fire hazard and maintains wax at correct working temperature (160° F or 70° C). Fumes from melted wax may cause respiratory damage which could have a cumulative effect. Caution should be

Fixation of Dyes

Some dyes in pastes (i.e., reactive and prepared vat) require a heat treatment to set the dyes. This treatment, often with an electric iron, releases fumes into the air. Layers of paper will help to absorb some of these fumes, but care must be taken to assure proper ventilation to avoid breathing these fumes.

Health Examinations

If one is working consistently in surface design with the dyes, chemicals, and other material covered in this text, there are several medical tests that should be considered. One of these is the test of Basic Pulmonary Function, which measures the amount of air put out by your lungs and the rate at which it is put out. Blood and urine tests can also be indicators of adverse effects of hazardous materials in your environment. These three tests could be part of a regular medical checkup and become part of a permanent long-term record that could be useful if health problems arise.

This section on safety in surface design is offered as a guide to the craftsperson who is unaware of the potential hazards encountered by engaging in the activities described in this volume. It is intended as the means to a reasonable approach to the use of materials, many of which have not been adequately studied, without endangering the health of the artist or those he has contact with. Awareness of hazards has increased, and it is hoped that new information will become available that will give the surface designer assurance that the activity engaged in is safe.

The dye formulas and procedures included in the final chapter have been selected for safety, color range, brilliance and fastness, ease of application, and availability. Consequently, not all of the dye classes previously described have been included. However, the range included will satisfy the needs of most craftspersons and can be used to dye a variety of fibers in a number of different processes.

Pretreatment of Fabric

Any fabric to be decorated with any medium must be washed free of sizing with warm water and mild soap, thoroughly rinsed, and dried. Some types of fabric need ironing after they are washed, while others will stretch out wrinkle-free when pinned to the work table.

Some media require that the fabric be further prepared before decorating by washing in a special formula which is vital to the success of the colors. The manufacturers of the media will supply directions for their products, and it is important to follow them for satisfactory results.

Fixation of Decorated Fabric

Almost without exception the media used in fabric decoration require fixation—the process by which the medium is permanently fixed in or attached to the fiber. It has been noted that some media have a higher degree of fastness than others.

Many fixation processes are basically treatments with moist or dry heat. Some dyes (Procion MX) can be fixed without the application of heat in both bath and paste forms. Dyestuffs applied in hot baths are fixed in the dyeing process. The general procedures described here are for the fixation of printed, painted, or cold-dyed fabrics. However, specific directions are given in Chapter 11 for each dye formula, and these instructions should be followed carefully.

After a fabric has been decorated with a dye paste, most of the dyestuff is held in the dried film of the thickening agent: very little will have penetrated the fibers. Steaming causes the printed areas to absorb moisture, forming very concentrated dyebaths in which penetration of the fiber by the dye takes place. Under correct steaming conditions the thickening agent prevents the dyestuffs from migrating or spreading outside the printed area. However, if the steam is too moist or the dye paste was improperly mixed, the film of thickener becomes so diluted that migration occurs. If the steam is too dry or the dye paste contained too much thickener, insufficient moisture is absorbed, and the dyestuff does not fix properly; much of it may wash away in the finishing process.

STEAM

Very simple equipment may be used to steam the dye-decorated fabric. The illustration on page 69 shows how an enamel preserving kettle can be used. Enough water is placed in the kettle to last an hour at boiling temperature. The rack which usually holds bottles or jars is turned upside down to serve as a shelf. Precautions must be taken to protect the fabric from accidental wetting, such as that from condensation on the sides and top of the kettle or spattering of the boiling water. Any spotting with water will cause unsightly bleeding in the printed areas. A layer of felt is placed on the shelf for this purpose,

and several layers of newsprint over it provide further protection. Neither the felt nor the paper should touch the sides of the kettle.

A layer of newsprint or thin cloth is laid on a table, and the decorated fabric is placed over it. The two are rolled together from end to end and then made into a coil with a string tied around it. This package is placed on the shelf with more paper and felt on top of it. Nothing should touch the sides of the kettle. The water should be boiling when the coil is placed in the kettle. The fabric should remain in the covered steamer for at least an hour. To ensure an even penetration of steam, the package of fabric should be removed, opened, rerolled from the other end, and tied up again. More water is added to the kettle, if necessary, and the fabric is steamed for another hour. The coil must be untied and unrolled immediately upon removal from the steamer. A large pressure cooker can be used in the same way as the kettle if a shelf is improvised.

The type and width of fabric are factors that must be considered when the use of an improvised steamer is planned. A 3-yard length of very fine batiste will make a comparatively small coil, while a 3-yard length of wide sail cloth will be much more bulky.

A steam cabinet can be built out of plywood and lined with galvanized metal. The interior should be sprayed with a rust preventative. The peaked roof eliminates the possibility of dripping caused by condensation. The steam is provided from below by water heated with immersion heaters, and perforations at the top of the cabinet ensure a flow of steam through the fabric. The quantity of steam required depends on the volume of the steamer. Approximately 1 quart of water should be converted to steam per hour for each cubic foot capacity of the steamer. (A 1-kilowatt heater converts about $1\frac{1}{2}$ quarts of water into steam per hour per cubic foot.)

The metal rack shown in the illustration of a steam cabinet (following) was made using a drawer slide for the side rails. Holes in the rack hold hooks to which the cloth is fastened. (T pins can be bent into hooks for this purpose.) The holes are set 2 inches apart to keep the fabric from touching itself, and the rack is placed so that there are 2 inches between the hanging fabric and the sides and ends of the cabinet.

A thermometer is inserted in one of the perforations in the top to give the inside temperature of the cabinet. The cloth is entered at about 200°F. It

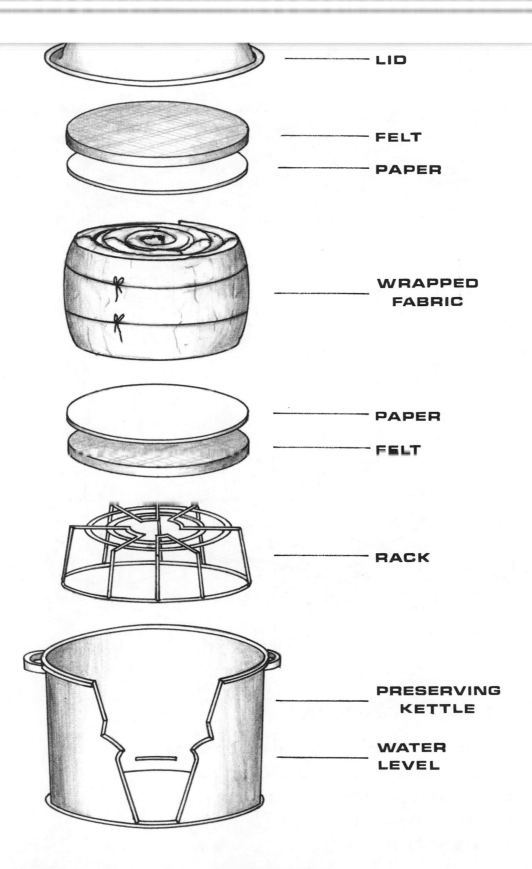

LID

FELT

PAPER

WRAPPED
FABRIC

PAPER

FELT

RACK

PRESERVING
KETTLE

WATER
LEVEL

IMPROVISED STEAMER

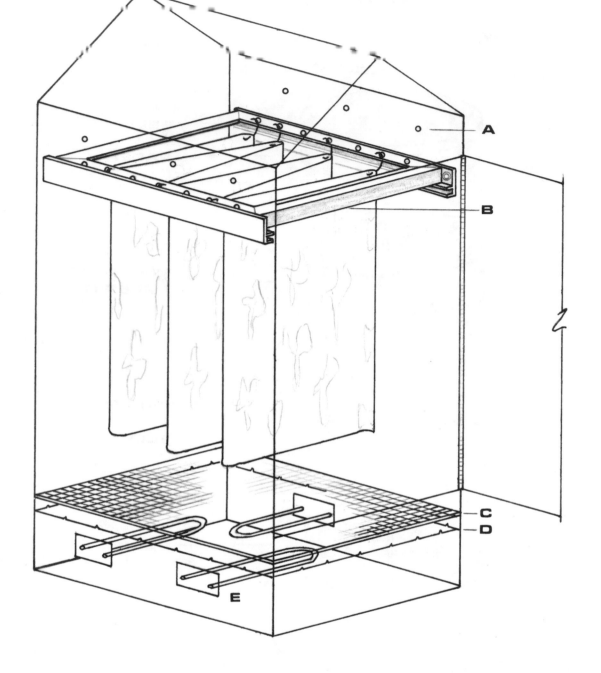

STEAM CABINET

A HOLES FOR ESCAPING STEAM

B SLIDING RACK TO HOLD FABRIC

C EXPANDED METAL SHELF

D WATER LEVEL

E HEATERS

door as quickly as possible. It will be noticed that the temperature is greatly lowered for a moment, but it will rise to 200°F. quickly as the water continues to boil.

The length of time the fabric must be steamed varies with the nature of the fiber, the weight of the fabric, the type of dyestuff, and the steaming equipment. The craftsman should experiment to find the time required for the best results. An efficient steamer with very hot, circulating steam requires less time than one which must reheat after the fabric is entered. The preserving kettle heats faster and to a higher temperature than the steam cabinet. However, the kettle holds less fabric, and there is more danger of spotting from condensation. Because the fabric is tightly folded in the kettle, more time is required for adequate penetration by the steam.

DRY HEAT

Many dyestuffs can be fixed with dry heat with equipment that is readily available. These include a laundry dryer set at the hottest setting, an electric iron, or an oven. A commercial ironer of the rotating-cylinder type is very useful in a school situation or a large production studio. It has a heated "shoe," thermostatically controlled, that rests against the rotating cylinder holding the fabric. In commercial ironing the fabric to be ironed is usually run directly through the machine between cylinder and shoe. For fixation requiring extended periods of heat the fabric is wound onto the cylinder with a clean pad cloth and allowed to rotate for the required period of time. A heavy fabric may be rewound with the opposite end to the outside of the roll and given a second heat treatment.

BATCH AGING

Procion MX dyes can be fixed by a process that keeps the dye-dampened fabric wet for up to 24 hours. This can be done by covering fabric on a table with polyethylene film for the period prescribed in Chapter 11. A state of dampness is essential for the fixation of the dye, and it may be necessary to sandwich the dye-painted or -printed fabric between layers of plastic. The fabric can be rolled in plastic film, making sure that dyed areas are not in contact with other areas of the fabric or that the film is transferring dye to unwanted areas.

evaporation, oxidation, polymerization, or a combination of these. In evaporation, the solvents pass into the air as gas, leaving the pigment dry on the fabric. Oxidation is a chemical process in which ingredients combine with oxygen in the air to form new compounds. Polymerization is also a chemical action in which the molecules of pigment form larger molecules that adhere to the fabric.

The fabric is usually air-dried as recommended by the manufacturer and then ironed on the reverse side for 5 minutes with a hand iron set for cotton. If the fiber will not stand this high temperature without injury, the setting can be lower, and the fabric ironed for a longer time. Some craftsmen use a bank of lights which is attached above the table in such a way that it can be passed over the fabric to heat one section at a time. The fabric may also be placed in a laundry dryer for about 30 minutes with the heat set at high temperature. Fabrics decorated with pigments can also be fixed by steaming if the temperature is high enough. (The manufacturer of the pigment will specify the temperature and time required for heat treatment.)

Fabrics printed with printer's ink should be air dried for 5 days, then dipped in a bath of 1 teaspoon of vinegar per quart of lukewarm water, dried partially, and ironed while still damp from the bath. Some brands of pigments do not require any treatment for fixation other than air-drying. Experiments based on the directions supplied by the manufacturer will show whether the proper combination of fiber, paste, and fixation process is being used.

Finishing

Fabrics decorated with dye pastes and in cold dyebaths require washing as a finishing process after fixation in order to remove excess dye, chemicals, and thickeners. The kind of washing—from gentle, cool baths to vigorous, boiling ones—depends on the tenacity of the thickener and the resistance of the specific dyestuff to washing and boiling. Washing will remove the thickener, which causes the fabric to be stiff, and a slight brightening of colors will usually be noted.

It is not necessary to finish the fabric immediately after steaming. However, once the finishing operation is started, it should be completed. The fabric is rinsed in cold water until all the loose dye is removed. (The finishing process will vary slightly depending on the dyestuff used. Additional treatments for each class of dyestuff are specified in Chapter 11.) It is very important not to let the fabric sit in water colored with the loose dye. The fabric is hung up to dry partially. Ironing it at this point is easier than dampening it again after it has dried thoroughly.

The craftsman should refer to the directions supplied by the manufacturer concerning finishing of fabrics decorated with pigments. Fabrics decorated with pastes containing a thickener should be washed in a detergent bath, rinsed, and dried. Most pigments, however, require no finishing. For future cleaning needs, dry cleaning is usually recommended, though most of the media will withstand gentle washing.

Preparation for Printing Techniques

Some preliminary preparation is required for the printing techniques of fabric decoration. It is much more satisfactory to attach an entire piece of cloth to a surface for printing repeated designs than to work on small sections of the fabric and move it. Some designs may be too closely repeated to achieve perfect alignment after repinning the fabric to the work table.

The size of a printing table will depend on the kind of printing the craftsman wishes to do. However, printing is usually done on yardage (3 yards or more of fabric). A table that is constructed especially for printing, therefore, should be more than 3 yards long to allow for several inches extra. It should also be at least 6 inches wider than the fabric to be printed; if space permits, a 60-inch-wide table will allow printing of all standard widths of cloth. A top of plywood, ½ to 1 inch thick, should be reinforced with 2-×-4-inch pine stock. Permanent legs of wood or metal may be attached; a height of about 30 inches is convenient. When studio space does not accommodate a table of these dimensions, the top can be set on sawhorses of the proper height, and the table dismantled when not in use. If the table is permanent, shelves can be built between the legs for screen storage. An ideal arrangement is vertical dividers that hold the screens in an upright position.

If the table surface is resilient and will give a little under the pressure of color application, more perfect color coverage can be obtained. A layer of felt or rug padding is tacked to the table top, a layer of muslin is stapled over it, and a back cloth of muslin is pinned over both with T pins. The back cloth is fastened tightly and straight with the table; the pins

are placed with the bar on the selvage and the point directed toward the center of the cloth, piercing the padding. The back cloth is a temporary base for printing. It is removed and washed after each use because the dyes often penetrate through the fabric being printed to the padding beneath. During printing the wet areas are likely to pick up any dry dye left in the back cloth.

The fabric to be printed can be pinned in place on the work table, or if the padding is protected with a waterproof cover, it may be adhered to the surface with gum or masking tape. However, since some dyes, such as the fiber-reactives recommended here, do not react favorably with the gum, masking tape is used to hold the fabric to the waterproof cover.

A measuring stick is used for a guide to mark a straight line across one end and along one side of the table with a soft pencil. The fabric to be decorated is attached with T pins starting at the side. It is pulled, stretched, and pinned until the entire side is fastened on the penciled line. To avoid scallops along the sides, the pins should be about 1 inch apart. The end of the fabric is pinned against the penciled line, and care should be taken not to stretch it out of shape at this point. The second side and end are then pinned by pulling the fabric straight from the opposite sides. Some adjustment of the ends is always necessary to take care of the fullness which results from stretching. Pinning the cloth straight and tight will help ensure a print on the straight of the cloth and will reduce registration problems caused by the tendency of the fabric to expand when wet and contract upon drying.

Some provision must be made for correct registration, or exact repetition, of block printed or screen printed designs. A very heavy T square, made of at least 2- x 6-inch pine stock, provides a simple tool to aid in the proper placement of the block or screen. Matching marks on the T square, table, and blocks or screen frames are referred to as registration guides.

To prepare for correct registration, a continuous strip of masking tape is placed over the pins along one selvage. Another strip is taped over the edge and along the bar of the T square. The dry block or screen is laid on one corner of the fabric so that it is adjacent to the taped selvage. The first horizontal row of prints will be here. The T square is placed above the block or screen, with the head fitted tightly against the table and the block or screen firmly in place against the bar. A pen or pencil mark drawn on the selvage tape where the edge of the T

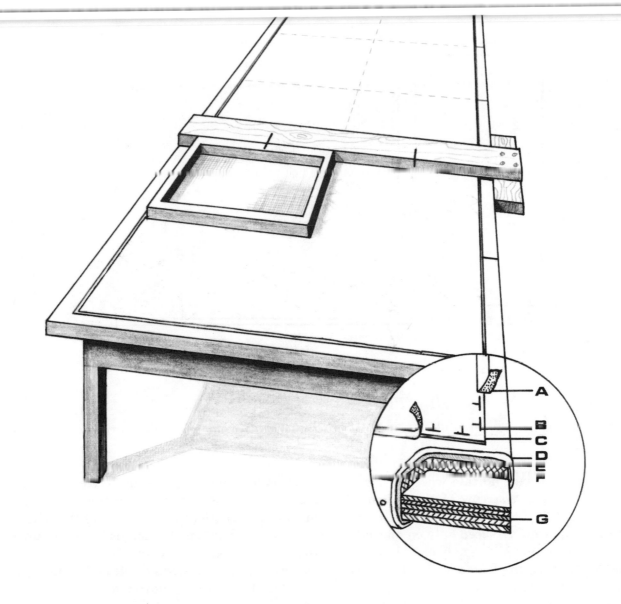

PRINTING TABLE

A MASKING TAPE

B T-PINS

C FABRIC TO BE PRINTED

D MUSLIN BACK CLOTH

E MUSLIN COVER CLOTH

F $3/8''$ FELT UNDERPADDING

G PLYWOOD TABLE TOP

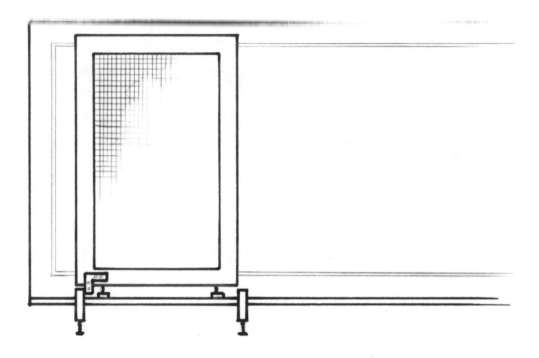

Top view of printing table and screen, showing the use of adjustable stops for registration.

square rests across it will indicate where to place the T square when the first row of the design is printed. (It should be noted that the registration marks for the T square are placed only on one side of the table.) A small piece of tape is placed on the back of the block or on the frame of the screen on the side touching the T square. Another mark on this piece of tape matched to one on the bar will be the guide for the first print of each row.

It will be realized that registration guides for the length of the cloth will be placed on the selvage tape, and those for guiding the printing across the width of the fabric will be matched to the marks on the blocks or screen frames and the T square. To determine the placement of marks on the bar for the second and following prints across the cloth, the width of the design on the block or screen is measured. To this figure is added any space to be left between prints. This sum is the distance to be measured and marked on the bar from the first mark and at succeeding intervals across the fabric. The mark on the block or screen will be matched to each of

these as the printing proceeds across the fabric. To guide in printing the following rows, the measurement of the length of the design plus the space to be left between prints is the sum used to measure from the first mark on the selvage tape for the second and following rows to the end of the cloth. During printing, the T square is moved to each of these as needed.

A second method of registration which is commonly used for screen printing is that of the guide rail with adjustable stops. This requires screens the width of the fabric. A metal guide rail is aligned with and attached to one side of the table. Sliding stops with locking devices are attached to the rail. The distance between the stops is adjusted to the length of the repeat of each individual design, and the stops are locked into position. Screws are attached to the side of the screen, resting against the guide rail. These can be moved in or out to further adjust registration and guide the frame in coming to rest against the stops.

5. Block Printing

Materials and Equipment

Artist's Spatula
Braycr
Flock
Linoleum-cutting Tools and Sharpening Stone
Linseed Oil
Pad for Paste
Plate Glass
Plywood
Rubber Gloves
Sandpaper
Saws and Drills (hand or power)
Sieve
Unmounted Linoleum
White Paint or Shoe Polish

Many materials and devices have been used for printing fabrics. One of the earliest techniques may have been dipping leaves and twigs in some color substance and pressing them on fabric. There is evidence of the use of incised bamboo, clay in the form of tablets and rollers, copper strips imbedded in wood backing, and, probably the most popular through the ages, the wood block. Linoleum has replaced the wood block for many craftsmen in the West. However, cardboard, plastic, rubber, cork, metal, and an endless list of other materials, either man-made or natural, may create decoration on fabrics. When dyes, paints, or inks are applied to the surface of a block and the block is stamped on cloth, a print results.

Design Potentials of the Technique

The unique qualities of the linoleum-block print will be realized if the craftsman takes advantage of the special characteristics of the material. In linoleum-block printing the shape of the cutting tools combined with the resistance of the material produces a typical "mark of the tool" unlike that of any other material. Practice on scrap linoleum will give a familiarity with this inherent characteristic of the technique, and the craftsman will soon find that ideas for prints develop from his experiments. The sharp, definite edges offer possibilities for numerous variations. Such effects as softly changing edges and values should be left for some other tools and materials to produce.

The cut-wood block offers a simple, direct approach to fabric printing utilizing readily available materials. Saw-cut wood shapes with plain edges and surfaces can be used to create interesting designs if attention is given to size, shape, and grouping. To experiment with the possibilities, a piece of paper may be cut and reassembled into a motif. A piece of wood of the same dimensions is cut and assembled in the same manner and glued to a backing to make a block for printing. Design is governed in some degree by the tools used for cutting the wood. The many possibilities for arranging the motif in repeat will become apparent with experimentation on paper or inexpensive fabric.

A variety of existing objects can be used for printing with little or no alteration. Great potential lies

Details of block prints showing the mark of the tool.

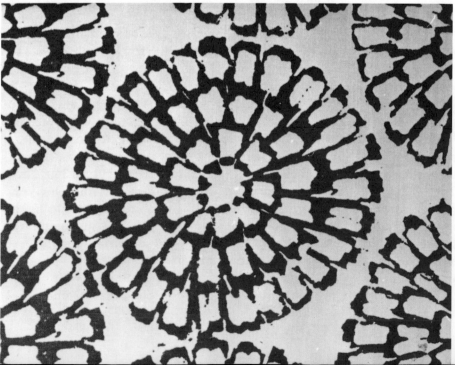

create a design.

The hard surfaces of most printing blocks resist dyes, creating textural effects in the print. This may rhomb textural effects can be created by using weathered wood or some other material with an uneven surface.

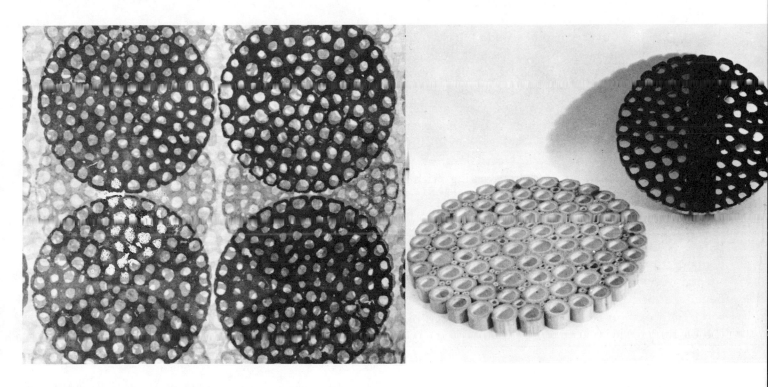

Found objects and the resulting prints.

Preparation

WOOD. The size of the printing block and, consequently, the size of the motif are limited by the manageability of the block in the printing process. A small motif can be repeated more than once on a single block to reduce the number of times the block must be stamped. It is difficult to apply color evenly to blocks larger than 12 inches square.

Shapes for wood blocks can be cut from plywood ⅜ to 1 inch thick or from solid wood at least ⅜ inch thick. A variety of handsaws are available which can be used for cutting the block, depending on the shapes required. When cutting by hand, the wood can be held in a vise. If power tools are available, blocks can be cut with circular, band, or jigsaws, and additional effects can be achieved with drills and other woodworking tools. Normal safety precautions should be exercised in working with all cutting tools.

In block printing the motif is reversed when printed; consequently a design should be reversed before tracing it on the wood. Tracing paper is convenient for reversing the motif because it can be turned over and the motif traced on the back. Soft pencil rubbed over the front of the drawing will serve as a carbon for transferring the design onto the block.

A rectangle of paper cut and rearranged to form a basic unit.

The shapes traced on plywood.

The completed cut-wood block.

Prints on fabric showing variations in placement. Textured areas result from unflocked shapes, solid areas from flocked ones.

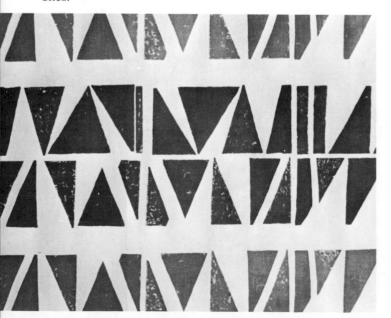

One side of the backing should be straight, giving an edge to locate against the guiding mechanism used. The backing may extend beyond the motif to form hand holds, or handles may be glued or nailed to the back of the block.

To prevent the block from absorbing water, dyes, and pigments, it is necessary to cover all surfaces with two coats of shellac. When dyes are used, the shellacked surface will give an uneven print or textural effect. For an even, solid print the block should be flocked. Flock is a finely shredded fiber which, when adhered to the block, gives it an absorbent surface. A special adhesive is available to hold the stamped onto it, thus picking up the varnish only on the printing surface. Flock is then sifted very thickly over the surface, and a piece of cardboard or wood is pressed over the flocked area to achieve better adhesion. It is left to dry for several hours before the excess is shaken off. A more absorbent surface is achieved with two or more applications of varnish and flock.

LINOLEUM. To make a linoleum block, a piece of linoleum the size of the motif is mounted on a piece of plywood at least ⅜ inch thick. Large sheets of linoleum can be mounted on plywood, and a complete block can be cut the size required. The backing

Cutting a linoleum block against a bolt head.

of the linoleum block should be shellacked in order to protect it from water, dyes, and pigments.

Before transferring the motif to the linoleum, the linoleum should be lightly sanded with fine sandpaper to remove its waxlike surface. The block is then coated with a light-colored, water-based wall paint or white shoe polish so that the design can be seen easily. The motif must be reversed before it is traced on the block in the same way as for the wood block. The block is now ready to cut.

Most studio accidents are caused by dull tools and the improper handling of tools. Linoleum knives are relatively inexpensive and should be replaced often. A sharpening stone should be a part of carving equipment. Whatever cutting tools are used, the fingers should be kept behind the blade at all times. A dull tool tends to slide, and a painful cut can be suffered if a finger is in front of the knife. For ease of cutting, a large bolt can be dropped into a hole in the work table. The bolt will turn as the block is shifted against the head. If the linoleum is difficult to cut with well sharpened tools, it may be heated slightly in an oven or other heat source.

Linoleum, like the shellacked wood surface, gives an uneven print or textural effect when dyes are used. For an even, solid print the block can be flocked in the same manner as the wood block. Shallow depressions and narrow lines or spaces between shapes may need to be cleaned out with the linoleum tools after flocking. This should be done after the adhesive and flocking have dried completely.

In all block printing, guides for registration must be indicated with marks on the back of the block for matching with those on the T square (described in Chapter 4).

Flocking a linoleum block.

on which to spread the dye or pigment is necessary. For dyes and most pigments, a pad consisting of a piece of ¾-inch plywood, double the dimensions of the block, is covered with a piece of resilient material such as rug padding or felt cut slightly smaller than the plywood. This surface is then covered with a heavy-duty plastic film which is held by staples or tacks on the reverse side, and over this a piece of thin felt or other absorbent fabric is fastened.

inch brush. The block is then stamped onto the dye-coated pad a number of times in several positions until the surface is evenly coated with the dye, but not so heavily as to fill up small depressions. The block is properly positioned on the fabric and firm pressure is applied evenly to all areas with the hands. Experimentation with small samples of the fabric will indicate the amount of pressure needed to achieve an even print. It may also be necessary to

Step-by-step procedure for linoleum-block printing with dye paste.

is essential to achieve a consistent application of dye to avoid dark and light areas in the finished print.

When printing with pigments, the color is mixed with the extender provided by the manufacturer and thinned to brushing consistency with a recommended thinner. The surface of the pad is then coated evenly with ink using a 2-inch brush. The block is stamped onto the pad as described above. Several trial prints should be made, varying the be used for block printing on fabrics. These inks are spread on a piece of glass with a metal spatula and rolled out evenly with a rubber or gelatin brayer. The brayer picks up an even coat of ink, which is then rolled onto the block. If the ink is too thick, it may be thinned with a few drops of linseed oil. Inking the block with several light coats is preferable to one heavy coating. The printing is the same as for dyes and other pigments.

Applying pigment to felt-covered pad for block printing.

Applying textile printer's ink to a linoleum block.

Linoleum-block print.

Blocks may be printed with printer's ink on acetate film, enabling the craftsman to reproduce the characteristics of block prints photographically. (The section on photographic stencils in Chapter 6 should be referred to for the procedure.)

Clean-Up

When dyes are used, cleaning blocks and equipment is easily accomplished with water, sponge, and a stiff brush. Solvents such as mineral spirits or turpentine should be used with pigments. A convenient method for cleaning blocks and brayers is to soak them in a large, deep cake pan containing the solvent. Depressions in the blocks may be cleaned with a stiff brush, and the equipment should be dried with a soft cloth. Proper ventilation should be available when using solvents.

Linoleum-block prints.

6. Screen Printing

Materials and Equipment

Absorbent Cotton
Acetate Film
Adhering Liquid
Bakelite Squeegee or Direct Emulsion Coater
Brown Paper Tape or Duct Tape (3-inch)
Brushes (soft)
Cutting Tools for Film
Developer
Developing Trays
Film Remover
Frames for Screens
Glycerin
Inks (opaque and waterproof)
Lamp (photoflood or carbon arc)
LePage's Glue
Liquid Wax Resist
Photo Emulsion
Plate Glass (¼-inch thick)
Presensitized Photo-stencil Film
Rubber-based Liquid Blockout (Maskoid)
Rubber Gloves
Sandpaper
Sensitizer (ammonium dichromate)
Squeegees
Stencil Fabric
Stencil Film
Stove Enamel
Tusche

Screen printing is the most recently developed of the fabric decorating techniques. It grows directly out of the Chinese stencil print. In stencil printing the design is cut in a sheet of cardboard, specially prepared paper, plastic, thin metal, or wood, and the dye is applied to the fabric through the cut-out areas. Screen printing works on the same principle, but the screen holds all the parts of the stencil together, and the printing medium is pulled across all the openings with one stroke, forcing color onto the fabric.

The technique has many advantages over the older methods of printing fabrics. It is much less laborious, because the size of the design or the number of repeats may be much larger than is possible with other methods, and once the design is on the screen, it may be saved and reused indefinitely. It has advantages for design because sharper and more intricate detail can be reproduced than with other techniques. With photographic screens it is possible to reproduce any graphic art work.

Design Potentials of the Technique

Since screen printing is based on the stencil technique, its design potentials will be evident upon examination of the various ways in which the stencil may be created on the screen. Each of the methods described below for blocking out some areas while leaving others open possesses special characteristics. Design ideas may result from these characteristics; on the other hand, certain designs suggest the use of specific stencil materials. The craftsman should become thoroughly familiar with the various stencil materials or blockouts that are available and with the solvents used to remove them. He can then plan to use them singly or in combination. The first decision must be which printing medium to use.

Stencil materials must be those which are not destroyed by the printing medium or its solvent.

Preparation

FRAMES AND SCREENS. If a ready-made frame is not used, one can be constructed. The most popular wood for making the frame that holds the screen is kiln-dried white pine, but spruce, mahogany, basswood, and boxwood are sometimes used. The important consideration is that the wood be as knot-free and as well dried as possible. For frames with outside dimensions up to about 15 x 20 inches, 1½- x 2-inch stock may be used. As the frames increase in size, the stock must become proportionately larger. A 20- x 30-inch frame should be made of 2- x 2-inch stock, and one measuring 30 x 40 inches requires at least 2- x 3-inch stock. Frames made of wood which is too thin will warp more quickly and drastically from the pull of the stencil cloth, from cleaning with water, and from general use and storage.

Several types of joints may be used in the construction of the frame. The frame must be rigid and have smooth edges and surfaces. Large frames should have metal corner plates for reinforcement.

A specially woven silk is commonly used for covering the frame, though cotton organdy, nylon, Dacron, or vinyon fabrics can be substituted. However, a good stencil silk, thoroughly cleaned after each printing and carefully stored, will last indefinitely. Domestic or Swiss screen process silks are available, and they are numbered, with XX following the numeral. The numerals denote the size of the mesh (the larger the number, the finer the mesh), and the X's the strength of the weave. (All silks used in the processes described here are XX weave.) For printing on fabric with pigments, 8XX or 10XX is recommended; for printing with dyes, 10XX or 12XX is suggested. It is convenient to identify indelibly on each finished screen the mesh size of the silk used.

Silks may be purchased in widths from 40 to 80 inches. It is economical to figure the most advantageous width for the size of the frame to be covered. Leftover pieces should be saved for covering small color-testing frames.

There are several methods for attaching the silk to the wood frame. It is most commonly done with tacks or staples, the groove-and-cleat, or the groove-and-cord. The last two methods require special equipment, and the beginner will find that stapling is adequate and the staple gun easy to manage without help. The objective is to have the silk as tight as a drum head and free from soft spots and ridges. It is helpful not to cut the required amount of silk away from the whole piece until the frame is covered, so that finger holds are available.

The silk is placed over the frame so that the selvage is parallel with a side and is about ½ inch inside the outer edge of the frame. Several staples are used to tack the silk to one corner. Next, the silk is pulled taut and straight and stapled at the next corner. Then the entire side between the corners is fastened, the staples placed about 1 inch apart and on a diagonal. Another corner is stapled after the silk is pulled taut and parallel with the edge; then the entire side is fastened. The silk is stapled to the remaining corner and sides in the same way. A second row of staples is placed around the entire frame, staggered between those of the first row and slanted in the opposite direction. Any staples which are not flush with the wood are hammered down, and the excess fabric is cut away.

The silk should be washed to remove any soil or size. A kitchen cleanser is especially suitable because the abrasive powder will slightly roughen the surface of the silk, preparing it to adhere more satisfactorily to the stencil.

Brown paper or duct tape 3 inches wide is used to protect the wood and fabric and to keep the printing medium from seeping out. Two strips of the tape, 2 inches longer than the length of the outside of the frame, and two strips, 2 inches longer than the width, are cut. They are creased by folding down the center, glue side in. Each strip is dampened with a sponge and placed on the frame so that half of the tape is over the staples and silk, and the other half is over the outside wood edge of the frame. The tape is smoothed and helped to adhere by rubbing with a dry cloth. The tape which extends

Adhering paper tape to the exterior edges of the frame.

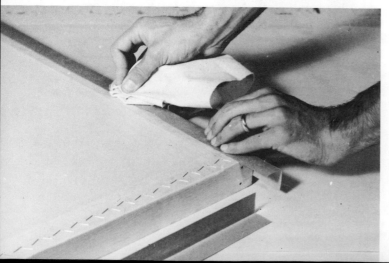

The frame is turned over, and corner pieces are made. Four squares of the tape are cut and folded in half in both directions; then one crease is snipped just to the center of each square. When one quadrant with a cut edge is folded over the other, the square will fit into a corner of the frame, making a protective seal.

More tape is cut, creased, and glued along the interior edges of the frame so that it adheres to both silk and wood. One or two strips of uncreased tape should be adhered across the silk on the two shorter ends of the frame, on both the inside and outside of the screen. This provides a reservoir for the printing medium that is 3 to 6 inches wide at each end. The wider reservoir is necessary for a large frame.

When the tape is thoroughly dry, all paper and wood surfaces are waterproofed with several coats of shellac or lacquer-proof blockout. The thick liquid is pulled across the paper and wood with a stiff piece of cardboard held perpendicular to the surface. The blockout should extend about ¼ inch onto the silk. If self-adhesive duct tape is used, it can be applied directly to the frame from the roll. This tape is resistant to water-based media but may be adversely affected by some solvents in pigment pastes.

Registration guides are now established on the screen. With the frame silk side up, a fine-tipped pen, waterproof ink, and a T square are used to draw centered horizontal and vertical lines that extend from edge to edge. If the silk is properly stretched and light pressure is used, there is no danger of damaging the silk. These lines will ensure proper placement of the design on the silk and aid in correct registration. Of course, registration guides must be marked on the frame to match with those on the T square (described in Chapter 6).

SQUEEGEES. The squeegee is the instrument used to force the ink or dye through the stencil onto the fabric being printed. It is a tool with a wood handle holding a blade of synthetic rubber. It should be an inch or two shorter than the inside of the frame it is used with, so that the entire width of the design is printed in one stroke. Several squeegees of varying widths, therefore, may be needed.

The handle of the squeegee should not be too large for comfortable use with one hand. If the edges are sharp, they should be sanded, and the handle should be shellacked to protect it during washing. The better squeegees have screws holding

It is very important to purchase squeegees which are made especially for textile printing. They have thinner and more flexible blades than those used for printing on paper.

When the blade of the squeegee is dull, uneven, or nicked, it will deposit an uneven amount of ink in printing. It may be sharpened with fine sandpaper, emery, or garnet cloth. These may be purchased in long strips or by the yard from screen process supply houses. The abrasive is fastened to a wood base, perpendicular to which an upright piece is attached. The squeegee is held against the upright so that a straight edge will result, and it is drawn back and forth until the edge is smooth and sharp again.

To avoid the inconvenience of having the squeegee fall into the ink between strokes, it is recommended that nails or small dowels be driven into the ends of the wood handle. These will rest on the frame and keep the squeegee upright when the printer releases it between strokes.

Stencils

Stencil materials may be divided into two general categories: those which may be used with dye pastes and those which may be used with pigments. The following tables list stencil materials which may be used as permanent and temporary blockouts and the solvents for them.

KNIFE-CUT FILM STENCILS. There are a number of films available for various printing requirements. All films are laminated to a thin backing sheet of paper or plastic which holds all the parts of the design not peeled away until they can be adhered to the screen. Plastic backing is preferable because it is more transparent and moisture-resistant than the paper backing. A film which shrinks or expands in damp working conditions can interfere with correct registration.

Good, sharp stencil knives can be purchased in a variety of sizes and prices. Handles are usually about the size of writing tools. Blades can be resharpened and used indefinitely. Some tools may be returned to the manufacturer for sharpening when their shape makes it difficult for the craftsman to do it himself. Knives should be kept in good working condition and protected from damage when not in use.

There are special tools for cutting lines of various

widths which strip away the film in the cutting. Other line cutters have two blades, which are adjustable, to cut parallel lines. There are compass cutters for cutting circles and swivel knives for irregular shapes.

In the knife-cut film stencil (lacquer-type or water-soluble), the areas to be printed are cut in the film and peeled away. The film, with the remaining design, is adhered to the screen, and when the backing is peeled away, a stencil is produced. The craftsman should not begin to plan the design on paper until he has gained some understanding of the characteristics of knife-cut film. To discover what these are, a piece of film may be taped to a drawing board, and whatever tools are available used to experiment. The textural effects possible and the variety of shapes, edges, and lines will be evident upon spontaneous exploration of the material and the cutting tools.

Printing Media	Permanent Blockout Stencil Material	Stencil Remover
Dye pastes	Lacquer-based knife-cut film	Lacquer thinner
	Lacquer-based liquid blockout	Lacquer thinner
	Lacquer-proof liquid blockout	Remover recommended by the manufacturer
	Photo emulsion on nylon	Remover recommended by the manufacturer
	Photographic film on nylon	Remover recommended by the manufacturer
	Plastic liquid blockout	Remover recommended by the manufacturer
Pigment pastes	Glue	Water
	Lacquer-based knife-cut film	Lacquer thinner
	Lacquer-based liquid blockout	Lacquer thinner
	Lacquer-proof liquid blockout	Remover recommended by the manufacturer
	Photo emulsion	Water with household bleach
	Photographic film	Water with enzymes
	Plastic liquid blockout	Remover recommended by the manufacturer
	Water-soluble knife-cut film	Water
	Water-soluble liquid blockout	Water

Temporary Blockout Stencil Material	Stencil Remover
Glue	Water
Lacquer-based liquid blockout	Lacquer thinner
Lacquer-proof liquid blockout	Remover recommended by the manufacturer
Liquid wax emulsion	Mineral spirits or turpentine
Plastic liquid blockout	Remover recommended by the manufacturer
Rubber-based liquid blockout	Peel or rub off
Stove enamel	Mineral spirits or turpentine
Tusche (liquid and crayon)	Remover recommended by the manufacturer
Water-soluble liquid blockout	Water

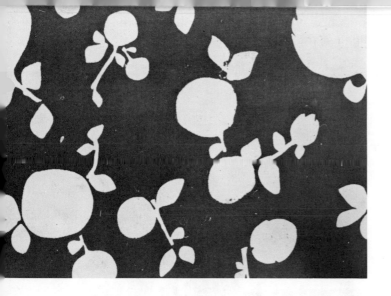

Screen prints made with cut-film stencils.

When a design has been thoroughly planned on paper and the repeat worked out, it is taped to a drawing board or other flat surface. A piece of film about 2 inches larger than the drawing is cut and placed over it and secured with tape. The film (not the backing) is cut with light strokes, as if the design were being traced. Heavy pressure is not needed and will only drive the edges of the film down into the backing, making it much more difficult to adhere it to the screen. If a white line is discernible on the underside of the backing, the pressure is too heavy. When the parts to be printed have been outlined, they may be peeled away by lifting an edge or corner with the tip of the knife. A corner with a clean angle rather than a torn one will result if the lines are extended slightly beyond the intersecting point. If the design has very large open areas, small slits should be cut in the backing to provide air vents and prevent buckling during adhering.

ble and toxic, and precautions should be exercised. To adhere lacquer-type film to the screen, the screen is prepared by wiping it lightly with adhering liquid. The film is laid on a thick piece of cardboard which is down, and whatever marks have been used on design, film, and screen to achieve perfect registration are matched. The cardboard will push the film tightly against the silk, ensuring adhesion.

"Worried Man," by Frances Butler, screen print.

the film with the wet cotton. It should be dried immediately by fanning and then rubbing lightly with a dry cloth. Another wet stroke is made, slightly overlapping the first, and dried in the same way. This process should be repeated until the entire film is adhered. The wet strokes should all be made in the same direction. Light spots show that not enough liquid has been used. These should be repaired after the whole film has been adhered, rather than soaking them with an immediate reapplication. Rubbing too heavily over a very wet area may melt the edges of the film, as will a surplus of liquid left too long before drying.

To adhere a water-soluble film, the screen is prepared by washing with a kitchen cleanser to remove any oil. The cut-film stencil is placed over a thick piece of cardboard which is larger than the film but smaller than the inside of the frame. The moist screen is then laid over the film, silk side down, and registration marks are matched. The screen is kept firmly pressed over the stencil, and a piece of cotton or clean rag soaked with water is used to wet thoroughly and quickly an area of about 10 square inches at one end of the stencil. The stencil is immediately blotted with paper towels, using a slight pressure. Wetting and blotting is continued until the entire stencil is adhered.

When the entire film has been adhered, the screen is set aside to dry for at least 30 minutes, and longer if possible. The backing sheet is removed by lifting one corner and slowly pulling it diagonally away from the film. It may also be removed by pulling from all corners toward the center. It is necessary to watch for any bits of the film which may pull away with the backing. To repair these, the backing is laid in place, and the screen is replaced on the cardboard pad. The process of dampening and drying is repeated over that small area.

After the film is adhered, any silk between the film and the edges of the frame is masked with a liquid blockout. Applying the thick liquid to the

face will cause the squeegee to lift and leave a poor print around the raised area. The frame is stood on a table and held at about a 45-degree angle. A small amount of the blockout is poured inside the frame in one corner and drawn upward over the silk with the cardboard, which is held perpendicular to the screen, so that a thin layer of blockout is deposited. This is continued from each corner until all the silk is covered.

Proper ventilation is also essential in using lacquer thinner to remove lacquer-type film. Working outdoors or with an exhaust fan is recommended. The solvent may be flammable and toxic. To remove film, layers of newspaper are placed on a table, and the underside of the screen is saturated with the remover recommended for the film used. The screen is then turned over quickly and set down so the film is in contact with the paper. More remover is poured inside to cover the entire area. Paper may also be placed inside the screen over the film. After a few minutes, the paper is removed from

Screen print made with cut-film stencils.

Screen prints made with cut-film stencils.

saturated with remover are used to rub over the silk on both sides of the screen simultaneously. This should remove all traces of the film. The blockout is removed with the recommended solvent in the same manner, and the screen is ready for the next stencil.

Water-soluble film is removed by soaking in water which contains a small amount of vinegar. When it begins to dissolve, it can be removed completely with a brush and warm water.

LIQUID BLOCKOUT STENCILS. The principle of the liquid blockout stencil is that a liquid called a blockout is used to fill in, or mask out, all areas of the screen through which the printing medium is not to pass. The design areas are either left open or are subsequently opened up to permit the passage of the printing medium. The simplest stencil is that which uses a single blockout, leaving the design areas open. However, a combination of two or more blockouts presents greater flexibility of application and thereby broadens the design potentials. The wide choice of liquid blockouts and tools for their appli-

screen process supply houses fall into four general categories: lacquer-based, lacquer-proof, water-soluble, and a plastic type. Precautions should also be exercised in the use of blockouts that may contain toxic or flammable solvents. All of these may be used with pigment pastes; all but the water-soluble may be used with dye pastes. Thus, the printing medium will determine the choice of blockouts. Each of the blockouts requires its own particular solvent for removal from the screen. Usually the solvent will also serve as a thinner. All blockouts should be kept tightly sealed, as they thicken rapidly through evaporation. In the water-soluble blockouts it is especially noticeable that various brands differ in viscosity. Some are similar to liquid clay; others are sticky. The craftsman can experiment with a variety of blockouts to discover what potentials each possesses for design. They can be applied with brush, cardboard spatula, sponge, syringe, or any number of other tools, or they may be dribbled, dripped, stamped, or spattered on the screen.

When liquid blockouts are used to reproduce a

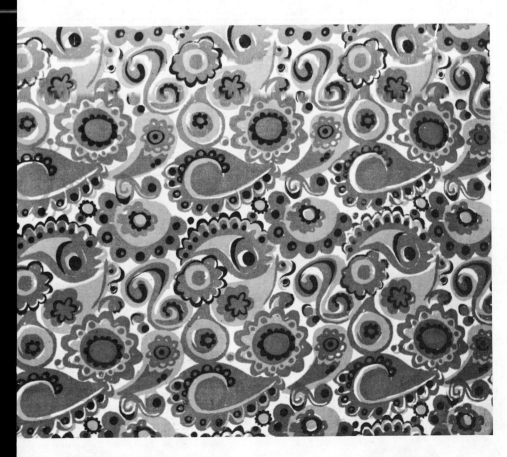

Screen print made with liquid blockout stencils.

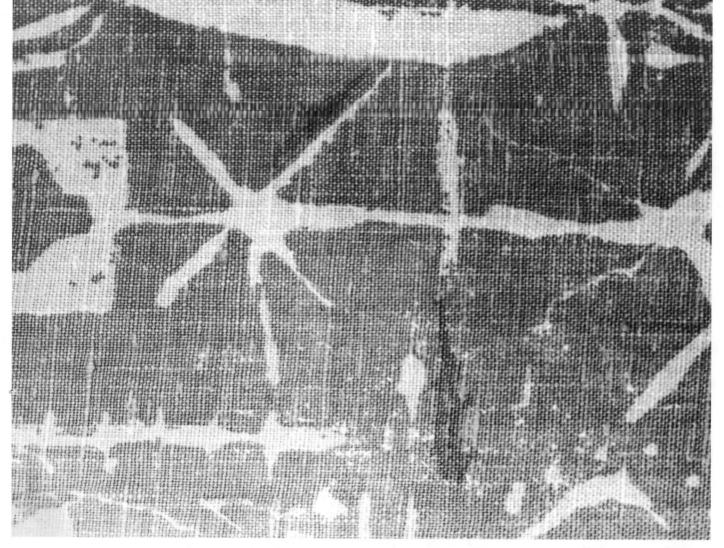

Screen prints made with liquid blockout stencils.

stencils for printing any number of colors with only one screen. The design and printing can be planned to take advantage of the overprinting of colors. When the design is traced on the screen and the registration marks are indicated, the blockout is applied with a brush or some other tool to all parts of the screen except those which are to be printed with the first color. After printing the screen is cleaned, and the blockout is removed completely. The blockout is then applied to all parts of the screen except those which are to be printed with the second color. Some areas of the first color may be left open for overprinting with the second. The second color is now printed. The screen is cleaned, and the blockout removed. The blockout is applied to all parts of the screen except those which are to be printed with the third color. Experimentation will show how many colors can be overprinted successfully.

The disadvantage of the single screen, single blockout method is that the stencils are removed each time, and only one printing of the particular design is possible. The same effect can be achieved by preparing as many screens as there are colors in the design.

Two blockouts may be used together, providing they require different solvents for removal. One serves to temporarily hold the design areas where the printing medium will pass through the screen during printing. It is applied to the inside of the screen, and two coats may be required to prevent the permanent blockout from attaching itself to the mesh in these printing areas. When it is well dried, the permanent blockout is applied, also to the inside, over the whole screen, with a piece of cardboard (as described above). This layer should be as thin as possible, yet fill the mesh completely. The thinness of the permanent blockout makes it more easily removable from the areas to be printed. This is accomplished by saturating the screen on both sides with the solvent for the temporary blockout and loosening the blockout with rags and stiff brushes. The permanent blockout will come away from the areas to be printed along with the temporary blockout. It is recommended that both sides of the screen be rubbed simultaneously. The screen is now ready for printing.

The craftsman will realize that it is possible to

is available for a multicolor design. However, it should not be attempted until tests have been made to establish how the various solvents will affect the various blockout media.

The first consideration is the permanent blockout which will resist all the other solvents. For example, the lacquer-proof blockout is not removable with water or the solvent for the plastic type, and most brands are not affected by the solvent for the lacquer-based blockout, so it can be chosen for a permanent blockout. The permanent blockout may be applied to some parts of the design area to hold the ground color of the fabric throughout, adding to the number of colors in the completed print.

After the distribution of colors in the design is decided upon, a water-soluble blockout is applied to those areas where the first color is to be printed. The lacquer-based blockout is then applied to the areas where the second color is desired, and the plastic type to the remainder of the areas to be printed. The permanent blockout is spread over the entire screen. When it is dry, the water-soluble blockout is removed, and the first color is printed. After the screen is washed and dried, the permanent blockout can be used to mask out the areas just printed to reserve that color. If the permanent blockout is applied to only a portion of these areas, additional colors will be created by overprinting. The lacquer-based blockout can now be removed, and the second color is printed. Again the areas just printed are masked out with the permanent blockout, and the plastic blockout is removed from the remaining areas. The third color is printed. Three colors have now been printed; with overprinting and some of the ground color retained, it will be apparent that eight or more colors can be attained with only three printing operations.

The advantage of this method is that a multicolor print is possible, and registration is more certain with only the one screen. A disadvantage is the slowness of the whole printing operation because the work on the screen is carried on between printings. Another disadvantage is that the stencils for each color are removed from the screen after the color is printed; thus the design cannot be printed again with those stencils. For this reason the craftsman may prefer to have a screen for each color prepared in advance. The resulting design will be the same, and the same print may be repeated as often as required.

A different stencil medium may be used for each screen for the various colors. The unique character of each type of stencil makes it possible to obtain a variety of effects. For example, one stencil may be cut film, which gives a sharp outline, the second may be lacquer-type blockout showing brushstroke effects, while the third may be plastic blockout applied with a sponge, creating textured effects. It should be noted that the standard film used for the knife-cut film stencil is lacquer-based and dissolved by the solvent for lacquer-based blockout, so these two cannot be used in combination. The water-soluble film, similarly, may be used in combination with all but water-soluble blockouts.

Several other materials can be used in place of or in combination with the commercial liquid block-outs. LePage's glue, thinned to 1 part water and 1 part glue, with a little glycerin added, will serve as a blockout that is removed with water. (It should be noted that this is not the household mucilage, but a glue which is packaged in cans and sold at hardware and art supply stores.)

LePage's glue is often used as the permanent blockout in combination with liquid waxes such as tusche or the wax emulsion used by ceramists for glazing. It is usually a wise precaution to apply two coats of the liquid wax, because it is thin in consistency. Solid waxes in the form of soft crayons and pencils add to the design potentials of the wax-glue combination. A popular way of using them is to lay the screen over a raised textured or patterned surface and firmly rub the crayon or pencil over the silk so that the effect of the raised surface is transferred to the silk. Glue is pulled over the entire screen, and the wax is washed away with its solvent and the help of a stiff brush. It should be repeated that the thinnest possible layer of the permanent blockout that still closes all the mesh of the screen is most desirable. Heavy deposits make the removal of the temporary blockout a tedious process.

The liquid waxes can also be used in combination with lacquer-based blockouts but are more difficult to remove than when used with glue.

Some rubber-based liquids (such as Maskoid) are manufactured for use as temporary blockouts. When dry, the permanent blockout is applied, and the rubber is removed by peeling and rubbing it away. It is recommended that the lacquer-based blockout be used as the permanent one with this temporary blockout.

Stove enamel can also be used as a temporary blockout. Though slow to dry, it is a thin liquid which is easily removed from the screen.

For short printing runs or for non-repeat designs, the craftsman will discover other stencil materials. Masking tape can be used to block out areas or to make a pattern. Cut or torn paper will stand up under a few printings with dye pastes and last for many more with pigment pastes. Pale-colored wax crayons can be used to draw on the silk, and the design left there for the duration of the printing, if dye pastes are used. (Dark-colored crayons are apt to stain the fabric.) Pigment pastes will dissolve the wax in the screen. It is also possible to lay thin flat objects or materials in place on the fabric to print over instead of attaching them to the screen. When the technique of screen printing is thoroughly understood, the liberties that can be taken with the materials become more evident.

PHOTOGRAPHIC STENCILS. The photographic stencil makes possible the use of designs with fine detail and other characteristics which cannot be reproduced easily, if at all, with any other stencil. It is much faster to prepare than other stencils and is more accurate, durable, and dependable.

Two types of photographic stencil are available to the fabric printer. One is a film which consists of a gelatin emulsion over a paper base. The other is the gelatin emulsion in liquid form. Stencils made with either of these are suitable for printing with pigment pastes.

The basic principle of the process is that when graphic art work done in opaque ink on a transparent surface is placed between a sensitized film or emulsion-covered area and a light source, the areas protected by the ink will remain soft and removable with water, while those which receive light are hardened and will not dissolve in water. The printing medium will pass through the washed-out areas.

The positive, or design to be printed, is applied to a thin transparent material such as paper or plastic which will not buckle when the ink is applied to it. The material most often selected is cellulose acetate, which is available in several thicknesses. Some acetates have one perfectly smooth side and one slightly grained, which will accept pencil sketching that can be erased without leaving a trace. The drawing must be done with an opaque ink which is easily manipulated with pen or brush, does not build up to a thick layer or chip off the plastic surface, and is absolutely light-resistant. These materials are available from photographic screen. In addition to brushing and drawing on the transparent sheet, an opaque medium can be applied by spraying, spattering, or stamping. Printer's ink can be used for the last. Opaque flat objects can be arranged under plate glass as a positive to produce the stencil. Some obvious ones are cut or torn paper, natural materials such as grasses, leaves, and seeds, and manufactured objects such as string, lace, etc. Other techniques of fabric decoration may be reproduced. Pelon can be tie-dyed with opaque ink and the resulting design reproduced. The possibilities are as varied as the individual imagination.

Screen print on vinyl, by Robert Kidd. The marbled effect was achieved with a photographic stencil.

PHOTO EMULSION STENCILS. Since you will probably find it difficult to remove some of the materials used for the photo emulsion stencil from the screen fabric, it is advisable to use Dacron instead of silk. A 12XX mesh is a good choice, since it should be as fine as possible but still permit a good print with dye pastes. Dacron is much less expensive than silk and resists many solvents and chemicals which will harm silk.

Each manufacturer will supply directions for the use of his product. However, the basic steps for preparing the photo emulsion stencil are as follows:

The screen is scrubbed lightly but thoroughly with a kitchen cleanser. The emulsion and sensitizer (ammonium dichromate) are prepared according to the directions, in a room darkened as recommended. The frame is then laid on the table, fabric side up. Emulsion is poured evenly over the tape at one end and pulled acros the mesh and off the other end of the screen. The tool used may be handmade or one sold for this purpose (called a direct emulsion coater). The tool is wiped dry, and an additional stroke is made, leaving a thin, even coat. The emulsion-coated screen is allowed to dry.

Screen print on vinyl, by Robert Kidd. The batik effect was achieved with a photographic stencil.

The method of exposing the sensitized screen will depend on the equipment available to the craftsman. It may be exposed with fluorescent, photoflood, carbon-arc, or other light source. Vacuum exposing units are made specifically for use in photo-screen making, but a light box, table, or other method can provide satisfactory results. It can be arranged so that exposure is from above with an overhead light, or a light table can be used so exposure is from below the screen. A very simple arrangement is the use of a photoflood lamp as an overhead light. The distance

acetate positive and the sensitized screen is an inflexible requirement. The emulsion-covered screen is placed over a thick piece of cardboard that is larger than the design but smaller than the frame. This will help ensure close contact. The positive is positioned face up inside the frame, and a sheet of plate glass ¼ to ⅜ inch thick is placed over it.

The light is turned on, and the screen is exposed for the time recommended by the manufacturer. This may be from 3 to 30 minutes. Since the strength of light varies considerably, the craftsman should make several tests for the best results. A small screen should be available for experimentation. If the emulsion is underexposed, it will not harden properly and much of it will wash away in the developing, leaving only a thin, pinholed layer on the fabric. If it is overexposed, the light will creep under the opaque ink and harden design areas, preventing them from opening up when the screen is washed.

The exposed screen is removed to a container of water or is placed under the water tap, where water at the recommended temperature will remove the unexposed portions. Both sides of the screen are wet, and a spray or brush can be used to clear the design areas.

The developed screen is laid on newspapers, and the excess water is blotted with more paper. When placed in an upright position, the screen will dry quickly.

A blockout is used to fill the open areas between printing areas and frame if the emulsion was not spread over the whole screen. An occasional pinhole may be found and filled with a water-resistant liquid blockout.

Emulsion is available that is resistant to both water- and solvent-based printing media. The supplier of the emulsion will also provide nontoxic solutions that can be used to remove the emulsion from the fabric after the stencil is no longer needed.

PHOTOGRAPHIC FILM STENCILS. The photographic film stencil makes use of a presensitized film over a plastic backing sheet. Many brands of film are available, each with its own developer, but the procedure is as follows:

The design is transferred to acetate with opaque ink, and the screen is prepared by scrubbing with a kitchen cleanser. The developer is prepared according to the manufacturer's directions.

A piece of the presensitized film is cut at least 2 inches larger than the design on all sides. Many films may be taken from their tubes only in semi-darkened rooms. The remaining film should be wrapped up and returned to the tube before any bright light is turned on. The film is placed backing side up on a flat surface, and the acetate positive, also with the backing side up, is positioned over it. A sheet of plate glass ¼ to ⅜ inch thick is placed over them.

The exposure time depends on several factors, including the kind of light used and its distance away from the film. These are matters for experimentation. Either a light table or a vacuum-exposing unit are also readily used to expose the film.

After the film is exposed, it is developed in the prepared tray of developer. The film is immersed quickly, film side up. It should be kept in motion under the surface for the time directed by the manufacturer. It is then transferred to a tray of water at the recommended temperature. The soluble areas will wash away. Some manufacturers recommend the use of a gentle spray of water to loosen the soluble parts, while others suggest a soft brush. When all design areas are open, the film is set by placing it in a tray or sink of cold water.

The film is removed from the water and placed film side up on a piece of cardboard which is larger than the design but smaller than the screen frame. This will ensure proper contact. The screen is dampened with a sponge and water and positioned over the film to match registration marks, and they are pressed together lightly. The screen is blotted gently with newsprint until all the moisture is removed.

The film should be allowed to dry thoroughly. Then one corner of the plastic backing is lifted and gently pulled away from the stencil. If there is too much resistance, more time should be allowed for drying. Any open areas around the film are filled in with a liquid blockout.

"Beach Grass," by Frances Butler, photographic screen print.

Preliminary tests of the printing medium should be made for correctness of color and consistency. Small screens and a matching squeegee for testing colors should be available. It is also important to have extra fabric for experimenting with color plans.

The order of printing should be planned in advance. To avoid picking up wet color on the underside of the screen frame, which is always much larger than the design being printed, the printing is not carried out in continuous order. It is usual to print the first, third, and fifth positions, etc. of the first row; then, skipping the second row and moving the T square used for registration to the mark for the third row, to print the first, third, and fifth positions, etc. This alternation is continued to the end of the fabric. Then the second, fourth, and sixth positions, etc. of the second row are printed; the T square is moved to the fourth row, and so on to the end of the fabric until all of the first color has been printed. The same procedure is followed for all the colors, and the same registration guides are used

Process of screen printing showing the alternating placement of the screen.

should be "wet-out" by printing it several times on a piece of spare fabric or absorbent paper in order to see that the dye is passing through the mesh properly. The screen is positioned over a sample piece, the squeegee is held 2 or 3 inches from the end of the screen in the area reserved for the printing medium, and a layer of the medium is poured across the screen between the upright squeegee and the frame. The squeegee will prevent the medium from flowing over into the design areas. The screen is held in place with one hand, and the squeegee is placed behind the printing medium and pulled across the silk with a firm stroke. Streamers of the medium should not be left behind. A good sweep of the squeegee should leave the screen with a clean surface. The printer should experiment in advance to find the number of strokes suitable and the proper pressure for the type of fabric being printed. Dyes print more successfully with the squeegee held at about a 45-degree angle, while pigments require the squeegee to be held in a more upright position.

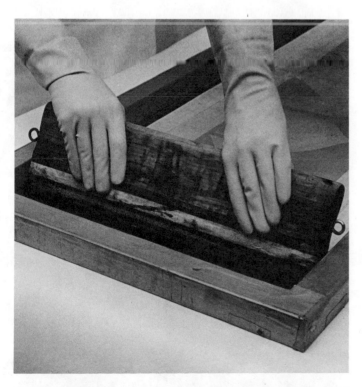

Position of squeegee for adding paste. The squeegee is held and pulled across the screen in the same position. Gloves should be worn for this process.

across the screen and the correct angle for the type of medium being used are necessary for achieving a level, well defined print. When this has been achieved, the first color run may begin.

The printing can be done in two ways. With the screen placed lengthwise on the table, the printer can pull one stroke, move to the other end of the frame, and pull the squeegee toward himself again. Another technique is to sweep the first stroke to the right with a backhand stroke and pull it back to the left.

After each print, the screen is lifted by raising one edge and peeling it away from the fabric. It should never be lifted straight up. To avoid smudges from the fingertips, which often pick up color in handling the squeegee, the wood handle should be wiped and the fingers cleaned often.

If it is unavoidable to interrupt the printing operation, the screen should be left where last printed. This will keep the mesh damp and unclogged for a short time.

After each printing, the fabric is left to dry thoroughly before another color is printed. This will prevent blurred edges where overprints occur. A fan may be used to speed the drying.

Clean-Up

At the end of each color run the screen is cleaned thoroughly. It cannot be overemphasized that printing media should not be left to dry in the silk. The screen is laid on newspapers, and all surplus color is scraped out of the screen and off the squeegee with a spatula or a piece of cardboard. If a dye paste has been used, the squeegee and screen are washed under the tap or with a hose and spray attachment. The latter is much more efficient and timesaving. A stiff brush can be used to help clear the silk.

Pigment pastes are washed from the screen with mineral spirits, turpentine, or the remover recommended by the manufacturer. The screen is placed silk side down over newspapers. A small amount of remover is poured directly inside it and washed with rags through the silk onto the newspapers. This is repeated with fresh paper and rags until the stencil and silk are thoroughly clean. Rags soaked with remover will clean the squeegee. Adequate ventilation should be provided. Solvents used for washup may be flammable and toxic.

7. Painting and Other Direct Methods

Materials and Equipment

Brushes (nylon)
Paint Rollers
Palette Knife
Rubber Gloves
Spatula (plastic)
Striping Tool

Painting and other direct methods for applying color to fabric are very ancient methods of decoration. Craftsmen have for centuries embellished fabric surfaces in a myriad of designs with simple existing tools. Today we think of this direct approach as one that affords great freedom and spontaneity.

Design Potentials of the Technique

The tools and methods used in direct methods of fabric decoration allow for a great deal of freedom in specific effects and allover design. The obvious result is a design which has no definite repeat of motif, unlike the designs created by printing techniques. In addition, the design is limited in scale only by the size of the fabric being worked on. The

Section of a coverlet or hanging, painted and dyed, India, 18th century. (Courtesy of The Cooper Union Museum)

since working directly on the fabric does not allow for major changes.

Since the tools used will directly affect the character of the completed design, it is essential to get the feel of the tools as a preliminary procedure. Brushstrokes offer a great variety of design potentials. An enormous range of brushes for painting color on fabric is found in art supply shops and hardware and variety stores. They can be chosen from fine-line widths to as wide as is maneuverable. They come with both long and short, soft and stiff bristles. There are round and flat ones, and tips may be shaped to give sharp edges, or they may be thick and stubby. Experiments with many kinds of brushes will give the designer confidence in his control of the tools. He will recognize how the character of lines and shapes are affected by the tool and how a motif can evolve out of some particular manipulation of that tool. The speed of the stroke, the wetness of the brush, and the position in which it is held are other variables in brushing color on fabric.

Spraying, spattering, and dribbling are other ways to apply dye to fabric, each with a specific effect. Sponges, rollers, cans, and similar devices offer new possibilities for types of lines and textures. The effects created by working on dry and wet surfaces also are among the potentials of this technique. Dye pastes inspire wet-on-wet experiments. They behave much as do watercolors on paper. The fabric can be dampened by spraying with water, or large brushes carrying pale color can saturate the fabric in preparation for the application of darker colors to the damp surface. Wetting the fabric with water will weaken the color subsequently applied, just as adding water or extender to the dye paste does. (If fiber-reactive colors are used, it should be remembered that the water applied to the fabric should contain the chemicals necessary to ensure that the ratio of ingredients in the dye paste is kept constant.)

Preparation

The design can be traced on the fabric over a light box or table. The design may also be transferred with a dressmaker's carbon and tracing wheel, or sketched directly on the fabric with a special pencil with fugitive color made especially for marking use in the textile industry.

decorated is stretched and printed on the back cloth.

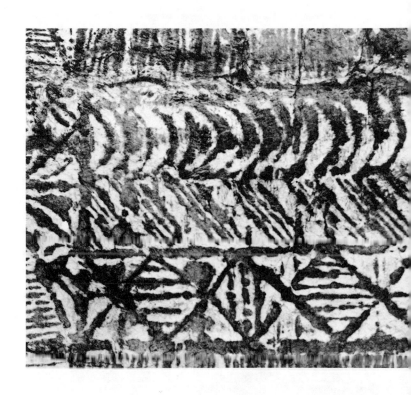

Painted cotton, Peru, ca. 1100-1400. (The Textile Museum, Washington, D.C.)

105

Details of painted fabrics, showing brushstroke effects.

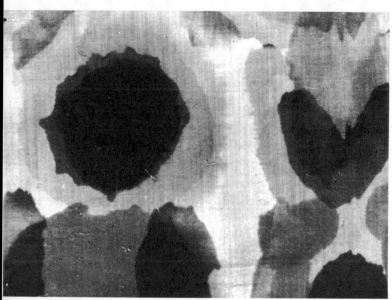

Painted fabrics, showing wet-on-wet effects.

for them and for the specific fabric to be decorated. The same media are used as in printing techniques, but they must be thinned for ease of application. Each type of fabric behaves in a characteristic way, and to achieve predictable results, some trials should be made. This can be done on one end of the fabric if additional length is allowed. The actual procedure varies according to the effects desired. Some of the possibilities, however, may be mentioned.

In painting, if dry brush effects and sharp edges are desired, it is necessary to let one color dry before applying another that will lie adjacent to or over it. On the other hand, if watered effects and blurred, running edges are desired, the work can progress without pause. If both wet and dry brush effects are desired, the background may be put in first and further detail added after this is dry.

Color may be applied through stencils of plastic, cardboard, or paper, or by brushing, spraying, rolling, or sponging. Plastic spatulas and palette knives, with their resilient blades, can also be used for spreading color or for linear effects.

If a stencil is used, precautions should be taken to keep the color from seeping under the edges. The consistency of the color and careful manipulation of the tool in application will avert such mishaps.

Sprayed color will assume a variety of aspects, depending on the device used and the distance the spray travels to the surface. It can be used to fill clearly defined shapes or can be employed for random effects. The color may be airbrushed to achieve solid, graded, or textural effects.

Rollers with various surfaces and in various widths can be purchased from paint supply stores or may be fabricated by the craftsman. The roller must have an absorbent surface to hold the coloring material. The effects produced will vary according to the amount of color carried and the freedom of movement exercised.

Sponges are available in various sizes and shapes. Again, the amount of color carried and the method of application will affect the visual results considerably.

Sponges and rollers can be used for stripe effects, though the need to replenish the color will not allow for long, unbroken stripes. However, these may be

It then is pulled firmly along the fabric surface from one end of the table to the other. In order to keep the can from being raised as it moves over the ends of the fabric, the fabric can be taped to the table with masking tape. A container can be held under the end of the table to receive the can as it is pulled over the edge. Guides for keeping the lines straight can be made from 2- x 2-inch pine stock of the required length, and attached to the table with clamps. Stripes may be varied freely in direction as well as in width. The width will depend on the sizes of cans the craftsman can collect, or two strips of masking tape can be used to make a stencil over which the can of color is pulled.

A striping tool set available at art supply centers provides a means of creating fine stripes or lines. It consists of a small bottle which holds the medium and also serves as a handle. A replaceable wheel is attached to the bottle, and as it rotates, it carries color to the fabric in very precise lines the width of the wheel. Several wheels of various widths are a part of the set. The choice of size and the maneuverability of the tool inspire diverse effects.

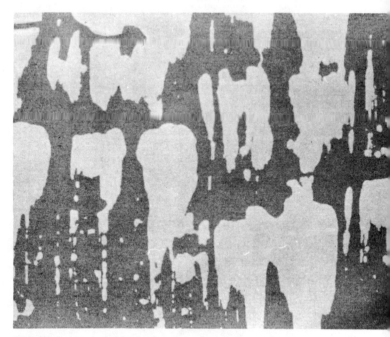

Detail of fabric, showing effect of discharge paste applied directly.

"Sleeping Earth People," by Lenore Davis, direct application and stencil, dye on cotton velveteen, quilted, 35″ × 45″.

8. Batik and Other Resists

Materials and Equipment

Brushes
Flour (wheat and rice)
Heating Unit for Wax
Laundry Starch
Liquid Wax Emulsion
Rubber Gloves
Scraper (plastic)
Stretchers
Tjantings
Waxes (paraffin and beeswax)

Batik is the term used almost universally to describe the process by which a substance is applied to predetermined areas of a fabric for the purpose of resisting subsequent dyeing. The dye-resisting substance most commonly associated with batik is hot wax. Actually, many other materials which will not melt or dissolve when the dye is applied to the fabric can also be used for resists. Other resist materials are basically rosins, fats, and flour pastes.

Design Potentials of the Technique

As with all techniques, the craftsman will better appreciate the scope of the design potentials if he experiments with the materials and tools before proceeding to sketches on paper. He may even devise new tools and materials which serve his purposes better, and experimentation will give him assurance in the control of the implements he chooses to use.

An infinite variety of all the elements of design can be realized with resists. Lines can be made with tjantings, brushes, or syringes. They can be stamped with tools the craftsman designs himself, thus expressing his individuality. The character of shapes will be the result of the choice and manipulation of tools: they can vary in size from the dot made when a wax-loaded brush or tjanting barely touches the fabric to large areas on which the wax is spooned, poured, or brushed with house-painting brushes.

More than one resist used in the same design will give contrasts of edges and surfaces. The craftsman who is familiar with the individual properties of the resists can achieve plain areas as well as crackled

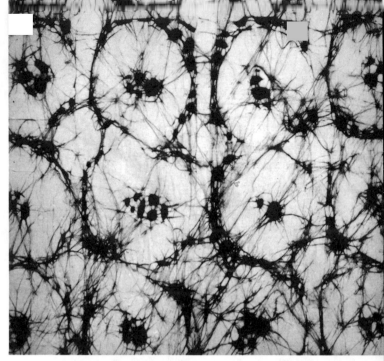

A variety of batik effects.

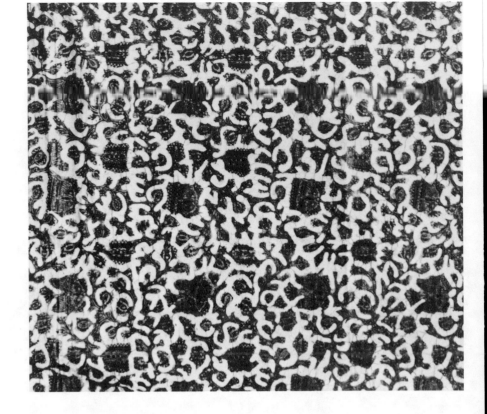

Batik on cotton, Java, 19th century. Repeated design made with the tjap stamp. (The Metropolitan Museum of Art, Rogers Fund, 1917)

ones in the same piece. Waxes can be scratched through or scraped; pastes can be combed. Lighted candles can be used to deposit melted wax by dripping. Waxed surfaces can be folded and crackled in specific directions to give emphasis to a design, or they can be crumpled and crushed at random. Various values of one color result from thick and thin applications of the wax because the dye will penetrate faintly in the thinly covered areas, especially with cold wax.

A further possibility with wax resists is to discharge existing color rather than to apply color. Wax is applied to those areas which are to remain the original color of the fabric, and the piece is placed in a discharge bath.

Preparation

Almost any kind of fabric is suitable for decorating by the resist technique if it can be colored with a paste or in a cold dyebath. Very thin fabrics such as silk and cotton organdy, batiste, and chiffon are often used because they accept both resist and dye so readily. However, the uses of these are limited, and very satisfactory results can be realized with linen of all weights, poplin, dress-weight wool, corduroy, velvet, and even terry cloth. The heavier

materials may require application of the resist from both sides if total resistance of the dye is required.

The design may be transferred to the fabric over a light box with soft pencil which will later be washed away. A simple design can be sketched directly on the fabric or transferred with a dressmaker's carbon and tracing wheel.

It is possible to apply a resist without stretching the fabric if something to which the resist will not adhere too stubbornly is placed underneath. In some parts of Asia the fabric is stretched over a table top that is covered with fine sand or china clay. Most craftsmen prefer to have the fabric stretched tautly on a wood frame. Thumbtacks or plastic-topped pushpins are recommended for fastening the fabric to the frame.

Curtain stretchers (such as those used after washing sheer curtains) may be used, and batik supply houses sell special stretchers which are notched so that their size and shape can be changed. Artist's canvas stretchers are useful for small pieces; for yardage, a large frame with cross-piece reinforcements can be made in the length and width the craftsman requires. Pine stock that is 1 x 2 inches can be used. A large stretcher is more convenient if it is either hinged or notched so that it can be dis-

HOT WAX RESISTS. The most familiar resist is hot wax, which usually consists of paraffin and beeswax melted together. Paraffin is a mineral-based wax produced by the petroleum industry. A half-and-half mixture is often used, but the proportions may be varied for special effects. The beeswax is soft, and a greater proportion of it will give a flexible surface which will not crackle readily, if at all. A dominance of paraffin will produce a crackle, but it is important to find the proportions which will produce the crackle without peeling. Too much paraffin in the mixture will cause it to crumble and fall away from the surface so that the dye reaches the fabric in areas intended to be undyed, and smudged effects are often the result. However, excellent results can be achieved using pure paraffin, though experimentation is necessary to arrive at a satisfactory formula. The size and type of design as well as the dyes used will determine the best wax for the desired results.

Paraffin and beeswax are easily procurable from grocery and hardware stores. The petroleum industry also produces a variety of other waxes, one of which is similar to beeswax and is much less expensive. (One example is Mobil #2305.) Since it is a bit softer, less is used in the mixture. A proportion of 3 to 1 is a good mixture for experimenting with the materials.

The addition of some kind of fat to the hot wax makes it more adhesive. This is the reason that some craftsmen use melted candle wax, which contains fat, for resists. A fat which can be purchased from drug supply houses for this purpose is stearic acid, a white crystalline substance obtained from tallow and other fats. A good mixture may be made of 5½ parts paraffin, 1 part beeswax, and 3 parts stearic acid.

Javanese batiks are often waxed with a combination of paraffin and rosin. A mixture for experimenting may be made with 1 part paraffin and 3 parts lump rosin. More paraffin will give a more brittle result.

A variety of utensils can be used to melt the wax and maintain it at the proper temperature. A small electric-pot-type heater of approximately 1-quart capacity with thermostatic control is ideal. An electric frying pan with a tin can open at both ends to hold tools is provided. Refer to Chapter 4 for specific suggestions.

The temperature of the wax is a matter for experimentation. A temperature of 160°F. is satisfactory, and in a container which has its own temperature regulator, this setting should be used. Every effort should be made to maintain the wax at a constant workable temperature. It is inefficient and frustrating to heat it, remove it from the heat to use, and have to return it in a few moments to heat again.

Wax that is too hot will ruin the bristles of a brush instantly. Brushes left standing in the wax against the very hot bottom of the container will be permanently bent or burned away at the tips. Wax which is too hot also tends to spread uncontrollably in the fabric. However, if it is not hot enough, the wax will not penetrate the fibers and will only build up on the surface of the fabric. It may then peel away in the dyebath, allowing the dye to penetrate.

COLD RESISTS. A variety of liquid resists are available. Some require special solvents. Some are plastic-resin-based and others are of a wax type. A wax emulsion used by ceramicists for glaze-resist effects can be used on fabric. A special fabric resist (gutta), made in France for use with special alcohol-based liquid dyes, can be colored to create special resist effects. The liquid resists can be applied from squeeze bottles or syringes with brushes or stamps to achieve a variety of lines and textures. They do not lend themselves to crackle effects inherent in wax.

PASTE RESISTS. Paste resists have included such ingredients as rice, bran, and wheat flours, salt, laundry starch, kaolin, and various gums. A very simple flour resist can be made with 3 tablespoons flour mixed with 1 cup cold water. The paste is placed in the top of a double boiler and cooked until it becomes semitransparent. It should be stirred constantly. While hot, it is brushed or spooned thickly over the fabric.

Another resist paste can be made with 1 ounce white flour, 1 ounce rice flour, ½ ounce laundry starch, and 1¼ cups hot water. The dry ingredients are mixed with a small amount of cold water until the lumps have been worked out. The hot water is added, and the mixture is cooked in the top of a

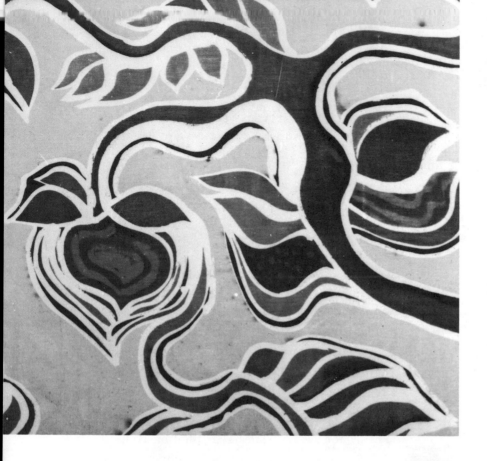

A variety of batik effects achieved with hot wax.

Detail of a batik panel by Ed Lambert. Resist lines are applied in wax with a tjanting. Dye application creates subtle shading and crystalline texture.

The fabric to be decorated is laid over wax paper or aluminum foil on the work table, or fastened to a stretcher which is laid on a table or propped on two objects such as sawhorses to hold it at a convenient height. If hot wax is to be used, the heating unit and container are placed safely and conveniently in relation to the work.

The procedure consists of applying resist to those areas which are to remain the color of the fabric, dyeing the fabric, and drying it. More resist is applied to retain some of the second color, and the fabric is dyed, dried, and waxed again, etc. (Dyes which contain alkalies, such as the fiber-reactives, cause the wax to begin to disintegrate after only two applications and two immersions in the dyebath. All waxed areas may have to be rewaxed, or it may be expedient to remove all the wax, put the piece through a detergent bath, and begin waxing again.)

The resist is applied to the cloth with whatever tools seem most appropriate for the specific design and fabric being used. Brushes of all sizes, shapes, and types of bristle are useful for all resists. A special tool used for applying hot wax to the fabric is the tjanting. It is a small metal cup with one or more spouts and fitted with a wood or bamboo handle. It is dipped in the container of wax to fill the cup and, with a bit of cloth held under it to prevent dripping, the wax is deposited on the cloth in dots or lines. The craftsman should experiment to find the most convenient way to hold the tool, as well as at what temperature the wax flows from it most satisfactorily. A syringe or a cake-decorating tube can be used as well as a brush for cold resists, and both hot and cold resists can be stamped on the fabric.

All resists are left to dry thoroughly before dyeing is begun. Fabrics treated with resists which contain rosin are usually left for several days before dyeing. To apply the color, the piece can be immersed in a dyebath after each waxing, or it can be left on the stretcher and the dye brushed or sponged on selected areas or the whole, depending on the nature of the design. If it is likely that the resist will not withstand the crushing and rubbing apt to occur in a bath of color, it is wiser to leave the piece on the stretcher to apply the color. In brushing on the

Use of the tjanting to apply hot wax.

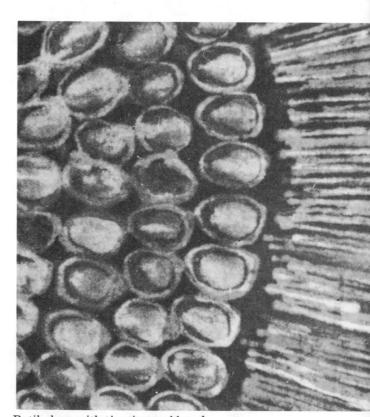

Batik done with tjanting and brush.

116

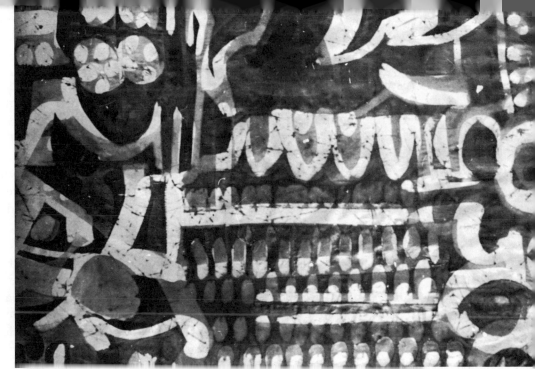

Batik done with a brush.

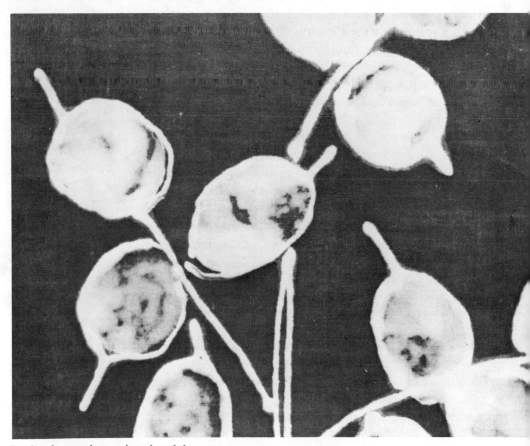

Resist decoration, printed and drawn.

uneven penetration is encouraged. When the dye is applied with a brush, it is more manageable **if it** contains a small amount of thickening.

When a crackle effect is desirable, more crisp, clean lines result if the waxed fabric is chilled before crackling. This may be accomplished by placing it in the refrigerator, dampening it under cold water, or leaving it out of doors during cold weather. The crackling can also be the result of crowding the waxed cloth into a dyebath. If the dye is to be brushed on, any crackle desired can be accomplished by pushing against the waxed surfaces from underneath or by removing the fabric from the frame, crushing it between the hands, and tacking it down again to receive the dye. More controlled crackling results from folding vertically, diagonally, or horizontally. Many craftsmen leave the crackle process until the last, and usually the darkest, color is applied. With this method dark veins of color spread throughout the piece and often contribute a harmonizing effect. However, it is possible to plan to reserve the lines in various colors by waxing over them after each crackling and dyeing.

In applying dye with a brush or sponge, it will be noted that excess liquid collects on the surface of the wax. If left undisturbed, these drops of color can be used to achieve another kind of textural effect. When a hot iron is used to remove the wax, the color is pushed down into the fabric and clings there. However, if this effect is not desired, the drops of color can be removed from a heavy deposit of wax. Paper is placed over the wax and ironed with a slightly warm iron. The drops will adhere to the paper. They can also be wiped away from the wax with a damp sponge or cloth, or the surface can be scraped with a blunt tool such as a plastic scraper.

Resist materials should be thoroughly removed from the fabric. A surface which retains wax will soil easily, and the dark rings left in and around wax-impregnated areas seldom enhance the design. The method of removal depends on the type of dye used as well as on the resist. The starch pastes may be removed by soaking the fabric in cool water and washing it in warm detergent baths, scratching and gently rubbing away the paste.

tween layers of paper, it is easier to remove **than the** hot wax. If the dyes permit, it may also be removed by boiling in a detergent bath, by repeated washings in warm water, or with cleaning fluid. Several methods are used for removing heavy deposits of hot wax. If it is important to save the wax for future use, the fabric can be laid flat and the wax scraped away with a dull plastic scraper (such as that used to remove ice from a car windshield). Slightly heating the surface will hasten the process. The wax will crumple and shred away from the surface if rubbed between the hands. Rubber gloves are recommended to protect the hands from the abrasion caused by this process.

The above methods are only the first steps in removing the wax, since there will always be some wax left in the fabric. The last vestiges are removed by one or more washings in a hot detergent bath with a final rinse or by dry cleaning.

Batik crackle.

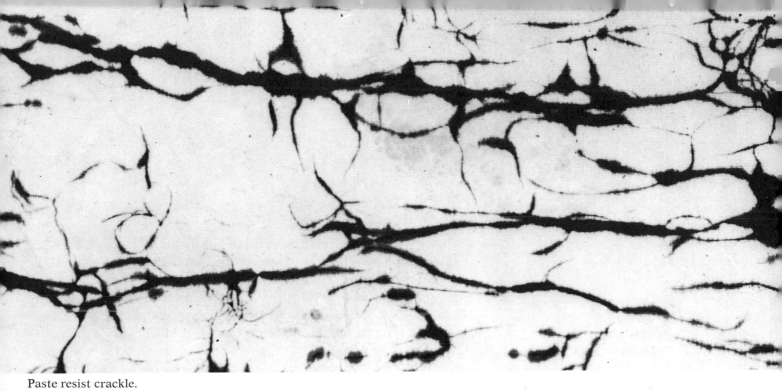

Paste resist crackle.

Discharge batik crackle.

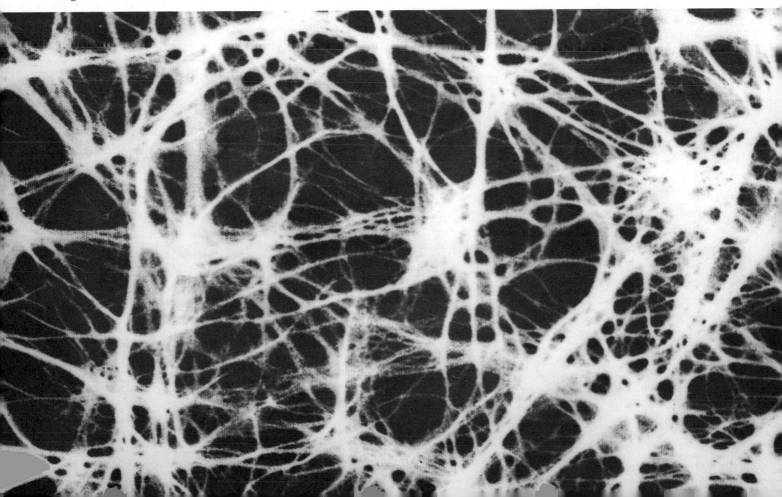

9. Tie-Dye

Materials and Equipment

Button and Carpet Thread
Cotton Cord (12-ply)
Raffia
Rubber Gloves
Sewing Needles
Sheet Plastic
Straight Pins
Wood Scraps

Tie-dye is a resist technique in which the pattern is achieved by dyeing it into the fabric rather than by applying it to the surface. The pattern is the result of reserving some areas by tieing, knotting, folding, or sewing them so that dye cannot penetrate. Other areas are either left free or loosely held so that they are colored.

Design Potentials of the Technique

Before making definite design plans for tie-dyeing, the craftsman should gather, fold, pleat, twist, and otherwise manipulate a piece of fabric in order to better visualize the design possibilities as well as the limitations of the technique. The effects of tieing the fabric in a variety of ways can be studied in small experiments. The size of the wrapping material together with the tightness of wrapping will affect the results. Several methods for achieving pattern can be combined in one piece. Cords for wrapping can be dyed beforehand and not rinsed so that color will bleed into the fabric. Textured effects can serve as backgrounds for definite shapes. Shapes can vary in size and character and can be arranged in bands, borders, or allover patterns.

There are enough accidental effects even with the most well planned and executed designs to make tie-dyeing an intriguing craft. It is necessary to plan the tieing and adhere to the measurements marked if a well organized design is to result.

Preparation

The fabric is ironed and spread on a table so the pattern to be followed can be marked on it. A soft pencil is used to mark lightly the widths of folds and indicate the areas to be tied or lines to be stitched. In some instances, as for the center of a circle, a dot will serve. A piece of thin cardboard is convenient for measuring and marking repeated shapes or sizes. A metal measuring tape, yardstick, or ruler may be used for accurate division of areas. Pins will hold arrangements of the fabric until they can be tied.

The craftsman will find that the position of the pattern in relation to the straight of the weave must be controlled for satisfactory design results. It is necessary to check the edges of the fabric to see that there is no slipping or pulling which will distort the pattern.

Procedures

TIEING. A 12-ply cotton cord, available at paper supply houses, is recommended for most tie-dye projects. It is strong enough to bind securely even the heaviest fabrics, and the large size of the cord is timesaving when wrapping large areas. Raffia is another strong material which is useful for tieing especially heavy fabrics.

Sheet plastic of a medium weight which can be purchased by the yard is used for tieing off wide areas that are not to be colored or to protect already dyed parts. (A thin plastic is easily pierced when manipulating the tied fabric in the dyebath, and a very heavy one resists secure tieing.) The plastic is wrapped around the pleated, folded, or gathered fabric several times and tied firmly with the cord. Immersion in a boiling dyebath does not harm it.

To start tieing off an area, the gathered fabric is held in the left hand, and the cord is twisted around it at least twice at the edge of the area to be tied off.

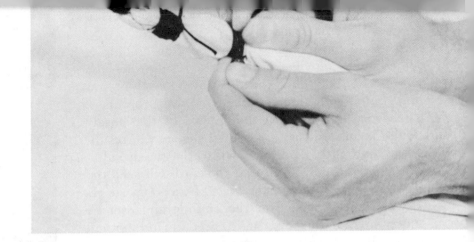

Fabric tied to create circular shapes.

Scissors are used as a bar to pull binding tight.

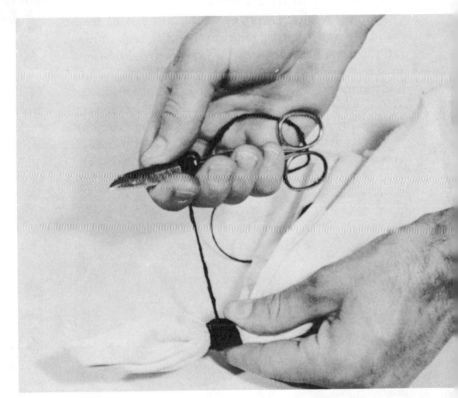

The short end of the cord is held under the thumb, 3 or 4 inches from the end. The long end of the cord is pulled tight with the right hand, and a knot is tied. The cord is then wrapped and pulled until the area is covered sufficiently, and then wound back to the beginning for the final knotting. If the dye is to be completely resisted, the area should be closely covered with wrapping, each twist of cord lying against or slightly over the last. Several layers will provide further resistance. The binding can be pulled more

tightly and the fingers saved from painful cuts if the cord is wound around a pair of scissors to create a bar for pulling.

If it is planned that the dye should enter between the bindings to create a repeated pattern, both the direction of the wrappings and the distance between them must be controlled. Wide or narrow bands at right angles to the length of the piece result from wrapping solidly straight across the gathered fabric, knotting, and cutting the cord, and repeating this

Sharp, definite edges occur when the binding is pulled very tight. Patterned edges result when the cord is knotted around the fabric a bit loosely at first and gradually tightened as the wrapping progresses. The dye will run down the creases of the loosely bound parts, and small repeated shapes will result, while the tightly held areas will resist the dye altogether. If there is doubt that the cord will keep the dye out of the fabric, some form of wax or paste resist can be brushed over the binding and over as much surrounding area as desired. (This method cannot be used with hot dyeing.)

Untieing is always left until the piece is at least semidry. Wet dye will migrate into the resist areas and destroy the sharpness of pattern if the fabric is untied. After dyeing and drying, the knots are cut and the cord is unwound. To avoid the possibility of cutting holes in the fabric, the cord is cut against the knot at the beginning or end of the tieing. The leftover end of the cord is pulled until there is enough space to slip the blade of the scissors inside. The cord is cut and unwound to the next knot, which is pulled away from the fabric and cut.

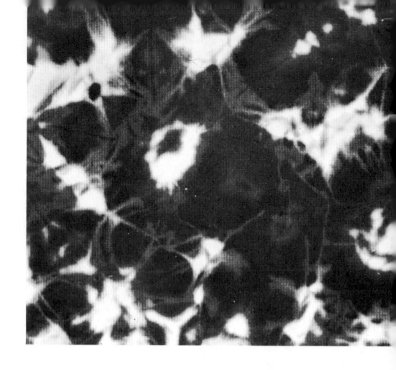

A variety of allover effects possible with tie-dye.

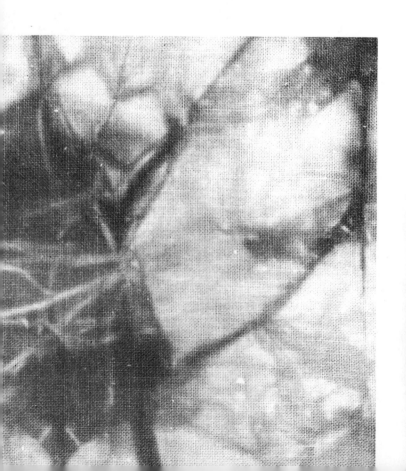

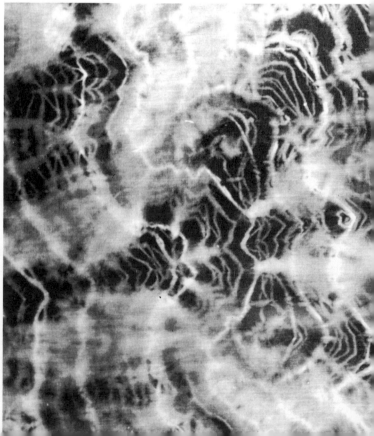

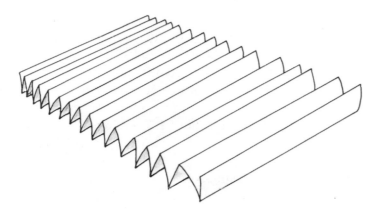

Fabric pleated and tied.

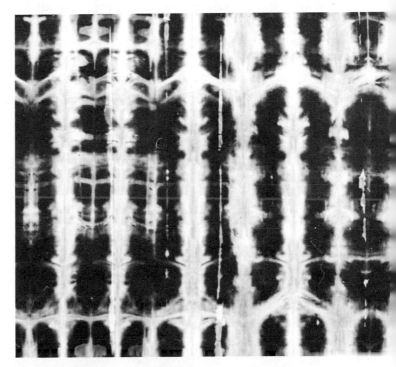

Patterns created by pleating, tieing, and dyeing.

PLEATING.   Pleating and tieing a length of fabric is one of the most logical ways to achieve a repeated pattern. A piece of paper can be folded to find what possibilities are presented by this approach as well as what problems will arise. Two methods of pleating should be considered. Beginning at one side or end, the piece is accordion-pleated to the other side or end. In this way the outer edges remain outside. If the piece is folded in the center and the sides or ends are brought to the middle repeatedly until the pleats are as narrow as desired, it will be found that the central part of the piece will have been brought to the outside. This is of concern because the areas brought to the outside will receive the heaviest concentration of dye.

   If the fabric is pleated vertically, the designs will be horizontal; horizontal pleats will produce vertical designs. Diagonal pleating results in diagonal design, but if the fabric is folded in the center and then the double cloth is pleated diagonally, a zigzag pattern will develop.

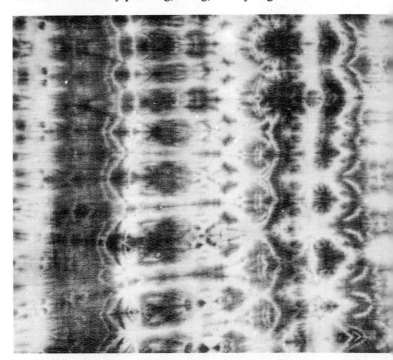

to hold the fabric in place until it is steam-ironed.

The pleated strip can be wrapped at intervals to create bands or stripes. The unbound areas will receive the first dyeing. When the fabric is semidry, some of the first color can be covered with wrapping to reserve it, while some of the first bindings can be untied so that these areas can receive a second color. Some of the colored areas can be left open to be overdyed by the second color. With two dyeings, therefore, there will be bands of the two colors as well as some bands with a third color created by overdyeing. The original color of the cloth under any of the first wrapping may give a fourth color. Further color effects can be achieved by brushing contrasting or darker-colored dye on outer edges. The location of these areas in the opened piece must be visualized so that scattered, unrelated effects are avoided.

The pleated strip can be folded at right angles to the pleats and tied to hold the folds in place as well as to create a variety of shapes. Other kinds of shapes can be made with the pleated strip by wrapping it around an object such as a piece of wood and tieing it securely. The edges pressed against the object will not receive the dye, while the outer surfaces will receive as much or as little as the binding allows. Twisting the piece as it is wrapped around the object will expose parts of both sides of the strip to the dye.

tics of weave, weight, and fiber.

The fabric is spread on a table and either gathered or pleated into a narrow strip. This can be done horizontally, vertically, or diagonally. The ends are tied very securely, and one end is fastened to an immovable object, such as a doorknob. While the total length is kept taut, the piece is twisted until it coils. The ends of the coil are placed together and wrapped with cord to hold the twist securely. This tight bundle will reject most of the dye except on the exposed areas. Larger pattern and deeper penetration of the dye may be expected if the least possible wrapping is used. Less pattern and less penetration will result from close wrapping, a broken pattern from rather open wrapping. It should be remembered that the direction of the wrapping will affect the design.

The bundle is immersed in a dyebath until the desired color and penetration are achieved. It is removed and allowed to become semidry before unwrapping and untwisting. The pattern probably will be scattered, and more twisting, wrapping, and dyeing may be done to bring undyed areas to the surface and to overdye some of the first color. The process is repeated as many times as necessary to attain an even distribution of color and pattern. Other colors can be introduced by brushing the dye over selected areas or by wrapping the bundle with predyed cord.

Steps in twisting a pleated fabric.

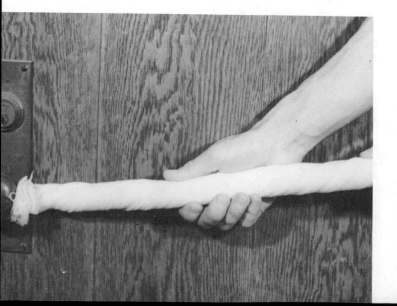
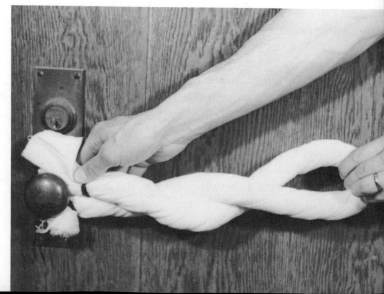

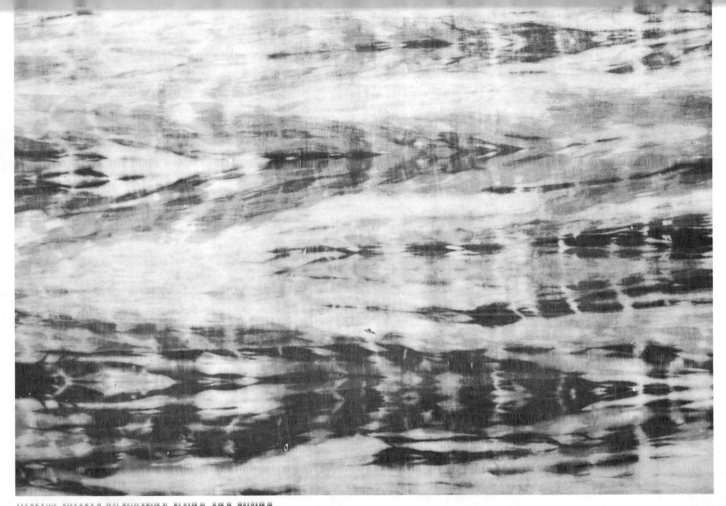

Pattern created by twisting, tieing, and dyeing.

FOLDING. Folding and dyeing without tieing can result in a controlled allover pattern of contrasting lines, shapes, and colors. A thin fabric which will allow the dye to penetrate quickly is recommended.

Very accurate measurements are required to achieve repeated pattern. The fabric is folded horizontally, vertically, or diagonally to create a strip. Further folding at right angles to the lengthwise folds will make a stack of rectangles or squares. Triangles will be formed if these shapes are folded diagonally. All edges should be ironed as the work progresses, preferably with a steam iron. Experimentation with paper is suggested before working with fabric. A special block-print paper or rice paper is ideal for this experimentation. Trials of a variety of folds and color applications will be helpful in design planning.

Steps in dip-dyeing a folded fabric. Gloves should be worn.

shapes. Dipping different edges may create stripes or plaids. An intricate pattern will result if each corner and edge is dipped in a separate dyebath. The piece can be tilted while held in the dye to produce still other shapes. When the desired depth of color is achieved, the fabric is removed and squeezed carefully and thoroughly to extract all excess dye. This can be achieved by pressing the dye-saturated fabric between layers of paper toweling or absorbent cloth. Be sure to discard towels or change cloths to prevent contamination by unwanted dye color. If several colors are to be used, the excess dye is removed after each dipping. It is not necessary to dry the fabric between dyebaths. When the dyeing is completed, the dyed piece is immediately unfolded and spread flat to dry. Touching up can be done with a brush dipped in dye.

KNOTTING. Knotting a pleated or gathered length of fabric will result in large, bold shapes. Thin fabric is more successful than others for this method of achieving pattern.

If a repetition of the motif is planned, an experimental knot will show the amount of fabric needed for one knot. The fabric is marked on each side of the knot, and when it is untied, a measurement of the space used is taken. A plan which allows for the amount needed for each knot and the space to be left between the knots is made. To achieve a pattern which will lie straight on the fabric, it is important to tie the center knot and then work toward the ends on each side, adjusting the fabric to keep the edges even at all times. Care must be taken to tie each knot in the same manner and then to adjust them by tightening or loosening, so that there will be similarity of shape and size. If the knots are arranged some distance apart, they can be dyed separately in several colors. It is also possible to hold the knots together above the dyebath and immerse only the spaces between the knots. After dyeing, the piece is allowed to become at least semidry before untieing if definite edges are desired. After untieing, more knots between or overlapping the first ones can provide further pattern and color variations.

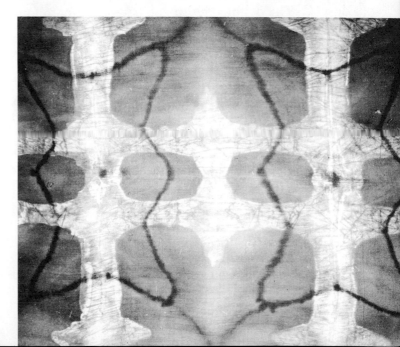

Patterns resulting from folding and dyeing.

the fabric while tieing to those as large as the width of the fabric allows.

To some extent the weight of the fabric will govern the size of the shapes: very small shapes require a finely woven fabric. However, even velveteen and corduroy can be tied for shapes on a larger scale.

The cloth is spread on a table and the plan for the placement of the shapes is indicated with penciled dots. The shapes can be arranged in an allover design that covers large areas, in stripes or borders, or they can be contained within other shapes. The dots indicate the centers of the shapes. For small ones a needle is used to pick up the dot and hold the center so that the fabric can be smoothed downward and tied as near or as far from the center as desired. The manner in which the fabric is pulled from the center point will influence the resulting shape. The larger the shape, the more care is required in distributing the fabric into even folds or gathers so that it can be tied into place. The distance from the center dot to the tie will be the radius of the circle or half the width of the diamond or square. Rings will result from bands of wrapping, while the tuft can be wrapped partially to create a patterned shape, or totally to create a solid shape. Tufts can be dyed separately in a variety of colors and then wrapped to resist a background color.

To make large, complex symmetrical shapes, the fabric is folded and pinned in place. Half the shape is drawn against the fold. A cardboard pattern may be used to outline the shape if an exact repeat is desired. The doubled cloth is pleated evenly following the outline and then wrapped carefully. The wrapping should be exactly on top of the penciled line.

Pebbles, seeds, plastic or glass objects, pieces of wood, cork, etc., can be tied inside a tuft of fabric to create a variety of shapes. An experiment will indicate the amount of fabric required for one motif, and allowance for this amount should be made in planning the placement of motifs over a large area.

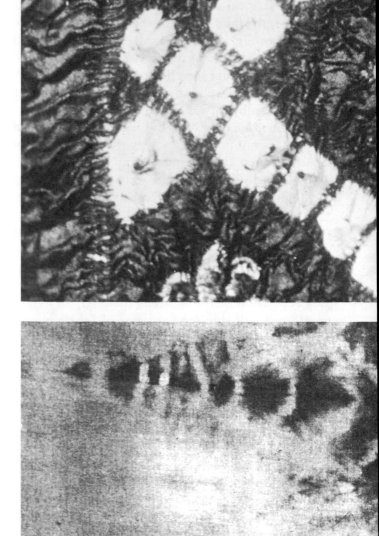

Shapes created by planned tieing and dyeing.

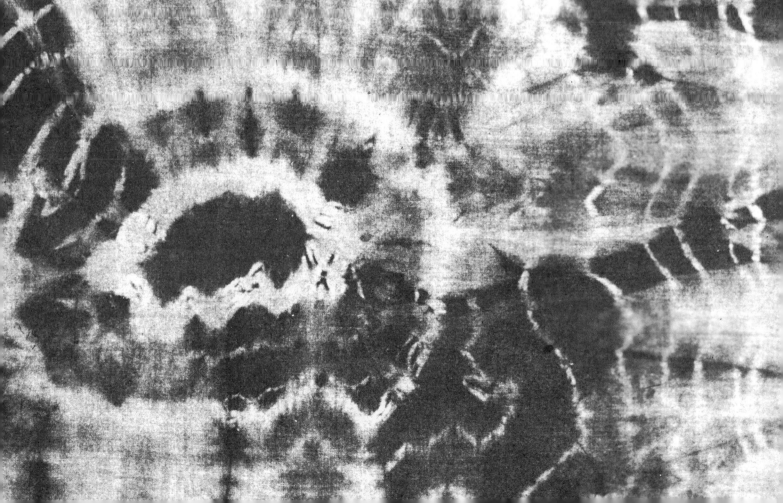

Silk sari with pattern resulting from stitching and dyeing, India, 19th century. (Courtesy of The Brooklyn Museum)

Cotton carrying cloth, stitched and dyed with indigo, Nigeria, 20th century. (Courtesy of The Cooper Union Museum)

STITCHING. Stitching is another method for creating areas which will resist dye. All kinds of motifs can be executed with either a running or a whipping stitch. Shapes can be abstract, such as stripes, diamonds, ovals, or circles, or they can represent natural forms. Intricate details can be produced as long as the shape can be outlined with stitches and pulled up tightly. The knot left at the beginning of the stitching is made large and strong enough to withstand the pulling necessary for satisfactory resistance to the dye.

Shapes are drawn or traced lightly in pencil on the fabric. If the shape is symmetrical, half of it can be traced against the fold of a doubled cloth. The piece is pinned securely, and running stitches are made through the two layers. Several rows of stitching inside the shape will give bolder effects and more complex patterns. The needle and thread from each row of stitching are left hanging until all are completed, since it is very difficult to sew on fabric which has some parts already gathered. The finished sewing is pulled up and held firmly while being fastened off. The stitches can be fastened off by tying the ends together or by backstitching. A single layer of fabric can be stitched, but it is more difficult to achieve a shape with definite edges in this way. Several rows of running stitches inside the shape will reinforce the outline.

The whipping stitch is more effective than the running stitch on a single layer of fabric. Very complex shapes can be drawn with pencil and a row of whipping placed over the outline with either small or long stitches. This will create patterned outlines. As the work progresses, the stitches are pulled firmly, but the gathering is left until all stitching is completed. In gathering whipped stitches, the head of the needle can be slipped under a stitch here and there to move along the excess thread and help pull it more tightly. The whipping stitch is usually fastened off by backstitching several times.

Stitches can vary in direction. The same line can be whipped from left to right and the stitches returning from the right made to cross those of the first row. More variety can be introduced by using running stitches in several rows and then whipping over them.

When several rows of stitches are placed close together, some can be pulled up to resist the first dyeing, and others tightened to resist the second. The first ones tightened can then be released to receive the second color, etc.

DYEING.   The most desirable dye will be one which gives the strongest color in the shortest time. Most pieces will be tied in such a manner that the bulk is reduced and only small baths are necessary. These can be given in bowls for cold baths or shallow pans for hot ones.

Because dyestuffs color at different rates of time, an interesting phenomenon occurs when two colors are mixed in the dyebath to achieve a third. For example, orange and turquoise blue may be mixed to obtain an olive green. After dyeing the tied piece, it will be found that the colors separate around the ties. The one that colors the fabric faster forms a halo on the edges of the green areas.

Sharper, clearer resists usually result from dampening the tied piece before entering it in the dyebath.

Running stitch, flat and drawn up.

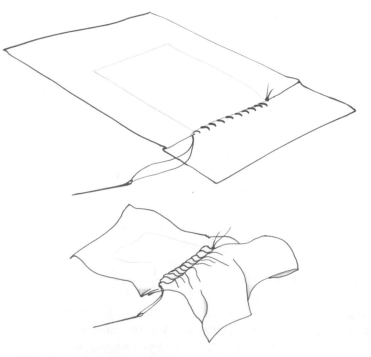

Whipping stitch, flat and drawn up.

The usual procedure is to begin with light colors and progress to dark ones in the dyeing. However, this is not an absolute rule, since it may be desirable to dye a light color after dark ones in order to color areas which were tied during previous baths.

Experiments with small tied pieces will help determine how strong the bath should be and how long the fabric should remain in it. The dyed piece may be left unrinsed until it has dried to allow the dye to penetrate the fibers more thoroughly.

A further possibility for obtaining design through tieing is to discharge existing color rather than to apply color. The tied fabric is placed in the discharge solution. Varying degrees of color value are possible when the action is watched closely, and the fabric is removed and rinsed when the desired result is seen. The piece can be tied further to retain some of the darker values and dipped in the solution again to obtain lighter ones. When as much color has been discharged as desired, the piece should be rinsed and untied immediately. The fabric should then be washed to completely remove the bleach.

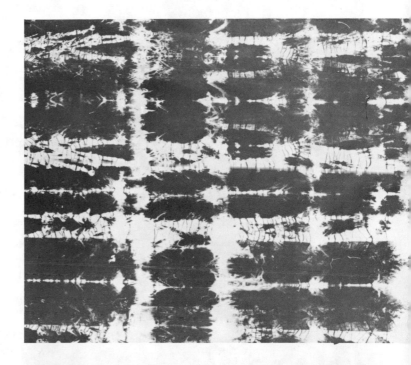

Effects achieved by tieing and discharging.

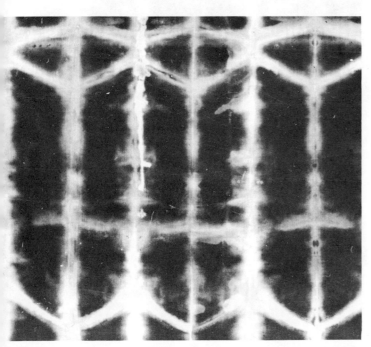

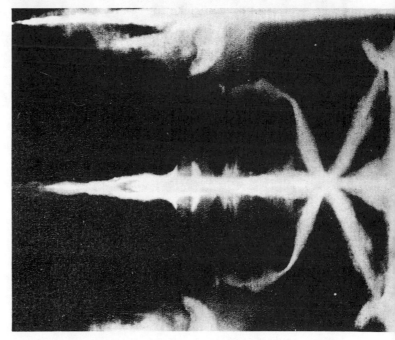

"Fandangle," by Pamela Scheinman, tie-dye (discharge), pleated, 52" × 45".

10. Transfer Printing

Materials and Equipment

Blocks (and other objects for printing)
Brushes
Crayons (special transfer type)
Gloves
Heat Source (iron, dry-mount press, or special transfer press)
Papers
   Solid-color transfer
   Patterned transfer
   Uncolored transfer (bond or white butcher paper)
   IBM copier II copies
   Color Xerox copies
   Newsprint
Rubber cement
Scissors

History

The principle of transfer printing on textiles is not a new one. One of the earliest uses of this process, in the late 19th century, was to transfer embroidery patterns to a ground cloth, usually cotton or linen. Printing inks containing shellac and colored pigments, often blue, were transferred to fabric by ironing. In this same time period polychrome prints, used for various decorative purposes, were transferred in a similar way.

The term "transfer printing," also referred to as "dry printing" or "dry dyeing," has several basic forms, two of which will be covered in this chapter. One of these, utilizing prints from a Xerox Color Copier, is of the "heat-melt" type. In this process a special resin-coated paper allows the image to transfer to fabric with the application of heat. The result is a pigment that adheres to the fabric as a result of the thermoplastic nature of the pigment and the resin. Most of the heat-transfer designs applied to T-shirts are of this thermoplastic pigment type.

A second type of transfer printing utilizing disperse dyes is a process that had its origins in the late 1940s but reached its first major application in 1958. A Frenchman, Noel De Plasse, developed the process of printing on paper with disperse dyes that could be transferred to fabric by means of sublimation. This occurs when a solid compound (disperse dye) vaporizes with the application of heat and reverts to a solid form again (within the fiber). The process became a commercial success after a Swiss-based company, Sublistatic S.A., exhibited its equipment and process in Atlantic City in 1969. This development was important for several reasons. First, it provided an easy method for printing polyester and other synthetic fibers (nylon, acetate, acrylic, etc.). Since only the dye transfers, becoming heat- and wash-fast, there is no need for fixation or washing-off steps in the process. Second, it allowed textile printers to stock printed papers in the patterns and colors of the current line and print the fabric to meet specific demands. This process also allowed the printing of delicate, detailed designs, some of a photographic quality, in a very reliable and easy manner. The materials and technology of transfer printing have become readily available to the studio surface designer.

Detail of a pieced work panel incorporating a polychrome transfer print, American, signed "Arthur 1887." Transfer inset, 5″ × 3½″. Collection of Glen Kaufman.

Design Potentials of the Technique

Since this process demands that the design or image first be applied to paper, many of the techniques of working on paper can be applied to transfer printing. The media available include disperse-dye crayons and liquid-dye paste supplemented by IBM Copier II copies.

The special crayons can be used for a wide variety of line, shape, and texture effects. The melting characteristic of the wax crayon can also be utilized, as well as its ability to create a resist when used with a liquid medium.

The liquid-dye paste can be used in the wide variety of direct methods described in Chapter 7. Screen and block printing on paper can also be used, and Chapters 5 and 6 should be referred to for specific ideas.

Preprinted papers in solid colors and a variety of patterns allow for a variety of collage effects. These papers can be combined with copier material to provide further opportunities for design exploration. Very detailed photographic imagery is possible with transfer printing to a degree not obtainable with other surface-design processes. A wide range of specific approaches and combinations of these are possibilities with transfer printing.

Preparation

Almost any type of synthetic fiber is suitable for transfer printing with disperse dyes if it can withstand the heat of the transfer process. Polyester accepts the dye most readily, but nylon, acetate, and acrylic are also very satisfactory. Tests on specific fabrics are rec-

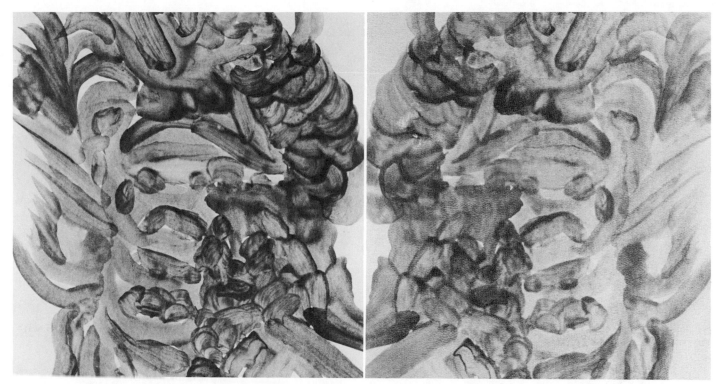

Disperse-dye paste is applied to the paper master to achieve brushstroke effects. The resultant print is on the right.

ommended. Fine-textured fabrics will pick up more detail from the paper than coarse ones, and woven fabrics tend to shift less when using an iron than knit ones. The "heat-melt" transfers using Xerox Color copies will adhere on any fabric that will withstand the necessary heat. All fabrics should be washed with detergent before printing.

A padded printing table is an ideal surface for heat transferring with an iron, providing it is covered with cotton or similar fabric, not plastic. If a printing table is not available, provide any table with a "bed" for ironing of a layer of newspapers with a clean sheet of plain newsprint on top.

Crayons, commercial transfer papers, and IBM Copier II papers are ready to use. The print paste is easily mixed, and direction will be found in Chapter 11.

A special word about plain papers used for transfer onto fabric: there are special transfer papers available from suppliers listed at the end of the book. However, tests have shown bond paper and white butcher paper (bought in rolls) to be equally effective in most instances.

Detail of "Shroud VII Leaves and Fishes," by M. Joan Lintault, printed, Color Xerox transfer-printed, sewn.

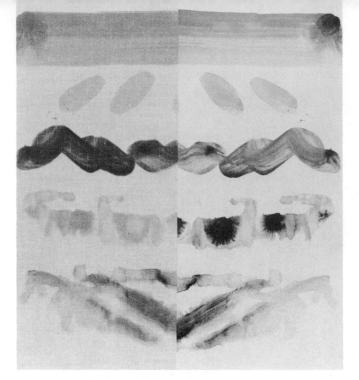

Dye paste applied to paper with brushes (right) and resultant print on fabric (left).

Transfer print on fabric made by rubbings of leaves with special crayons onto paper.

Procedures

CRAYONS

The special disperse-dye crayons can be used in a number of ways including the transfer of textures by means of rubbing. Melting small bits of crayon on the transfer paper or melting whole crayons and brushing them on the paper are other possible approaches. For fine lines one can make a sort of "carbon paper" by first applying a thin layer of chalk to paper, then a solid layer of crayon. Then, with a second sheet of paper over the carbon, draw fine lines with a ballpoint pen, which will pick up the crayon in a fine line.

When working with crayon be sure to remove all the bits of wax that usually flake off. If this is not done, the flakes will print, creating small dots where they may not be wanted. Clean these bits of wax off away from the fabric to be printed or contamination will result.

DYE PASTE

The disperse dye in paste form can be applied with brushes, blocks, screens, sprays, or any other way conceivable. Brushstrokes and many other textures obtained will transfer with varying degrees of fidelity. This seems to be related to the amount of dye paste deposited on the paper by the brush or other tool. On the other hand, details transferred from commercially printed transfer paper are reproduced on fabric with a high degree of fidelity. Commercially prepared solvent-based disperse-dye pastes are also available. Washup is done with mineral spirits or a similar solvent that requires adequate ventilation.

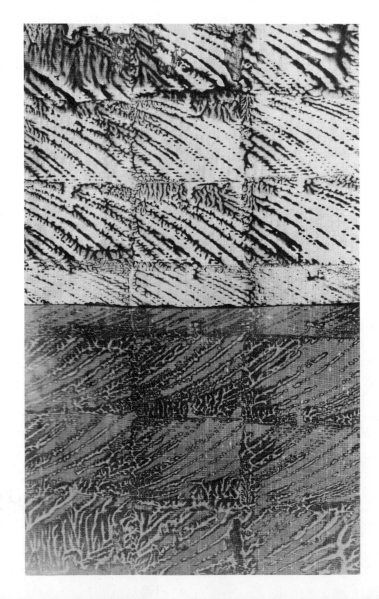

SCREEN PRINTING

The dye paste can be used for screen printing; but, since it is aqueous-based, it will tend to make paper cockle (wrinkle). To minimize this problem, a heavy white butcher paper is recommended. If the paper can be weighted on a table, cockling can be reduced further. Cut the paper long enough to reach the floor at both ends of the printing table, then create a loop in the paper of "8–12" at each end with a strong adhesive tape. Place a pipe or heavy rod in each loop that will hold the paper flat to the surface. The solvent-based pastes can also be used for screen printing, eliminating the problem of cockled paper.

Color

All colors of dye paste can be intermixed to achieve a wide palette. Water and/or clear paste can be added to achieve tints or watered effects.

A major problem in working with disperse dyes is that they change color dramatically when heated and transferred to the fabric. Extensive working and testing is essential for any degree of color control. Most colors, prior to sublimation transfer, tend to be dark and appear as shades or tones. They can, however, give brilliant colors of high intensity when heated. The temperature of the heat source, the length of time the heat is applied, and the fiber of the fabric being printed can all affect the final transferred color. A pattern book of colors on various fabrics is an essential resource if the craftsperson is going to work extensively in this technique and exercise control over color.

Overprinting of colors in the transfer process also poses special problems. Generally speaking, if two colors of equal strength are applied one over the other, the one applied *last* on the paper and *first* on the fabric will tend to dominate. Trials are also essential for overprinting. For example, if a blue is applied first to the paper and a red applied over it, the resultant color will be red-violet. All dye paste should be thoroughly dry before transfer printing is attempted.

IBM Copier II Prints

Copies made on the IBM Copier II machine will pick up dye from the commercially printed or hand-screen-printed paper in the configuration of the copier image. More color is picked up on the black-line or solid areas than on the unprinted white ground, but note that color is transferred to the entire surface of the copier paper. If shapes are cut out, careful cutting is essential.

Block print with disperse-dye paste on commercially printed paper with a linen-weave design (top) and the resultant print on fabric (bottom).

To transfer the color to the copier print, place a clean piece of newsprint over the padded table surface or "bed" prepared if an iron is being used. Lay the copier cutout face up and cover with a piece of color transfer paper facedown so color and image are in contact. Place another piece of clean newsprint over all. The paper containing the dye is always closest to the heat source in order to force the dye down into the copier paper or fabric. If a press is being used, make the same "sandwiched" layers described.

Heat dry-mount press or transfer press to 350°F. If an iron is being used, "cotton" setting is recommended. A nonsteam iron is preferred, since it has no holes on the sole which may transfer if the iron is not kept in motion. Place the "sandwich" in the press 30 seconds. Peel copy away from colored paper. If there is any problem of adhesion between copy and colored paper, leaving small white areas on the copy, allow the papers to cool completely (5–10 minutes) before peeling them apart.

Xerox Color Copier Prints

In order to achieve a transfer print from a Xerox Color copy, a special transfer paper must be used in the machine. Check to see if a local copy service stocks the special paper. If not, ask if copies can be made on the paper if it is furnished. Some copy services may be unfamiliar with the use of transfer papers and will be unwilling to try. There are many problems in using the special paper in the machines, as it has a slick surface and will not always be carried through properly. Some paper is subject to humidity, and this can create problems. Sometimes the rollers in the machine that move the paper need special cleaning. Once all these problems are solved, the possibilities are unlimited.

For transfer onto fabric follow the instructions provided with the paper. Dry-mount press, transfer press, or electric iron can be used. A nonsteam iron is preferred for reasons explained previously. A setting of 149°C (300°F) for 30 seconds is recommended with some papers. Set an iron at "wool" setting. Experimentation with temperature and contact time is essential. Always try a test strip before embarking on a major project.

Adhesion between paper and fabric can be quite strong. Begin peeling while work is hot and reheat if necessary either to complete transfer or to remove paper from fabric. Transfer of the image should be quite complete with only a trace left on the paper. If using an iron, reheat portions as needed to complete transfer or remove paper.

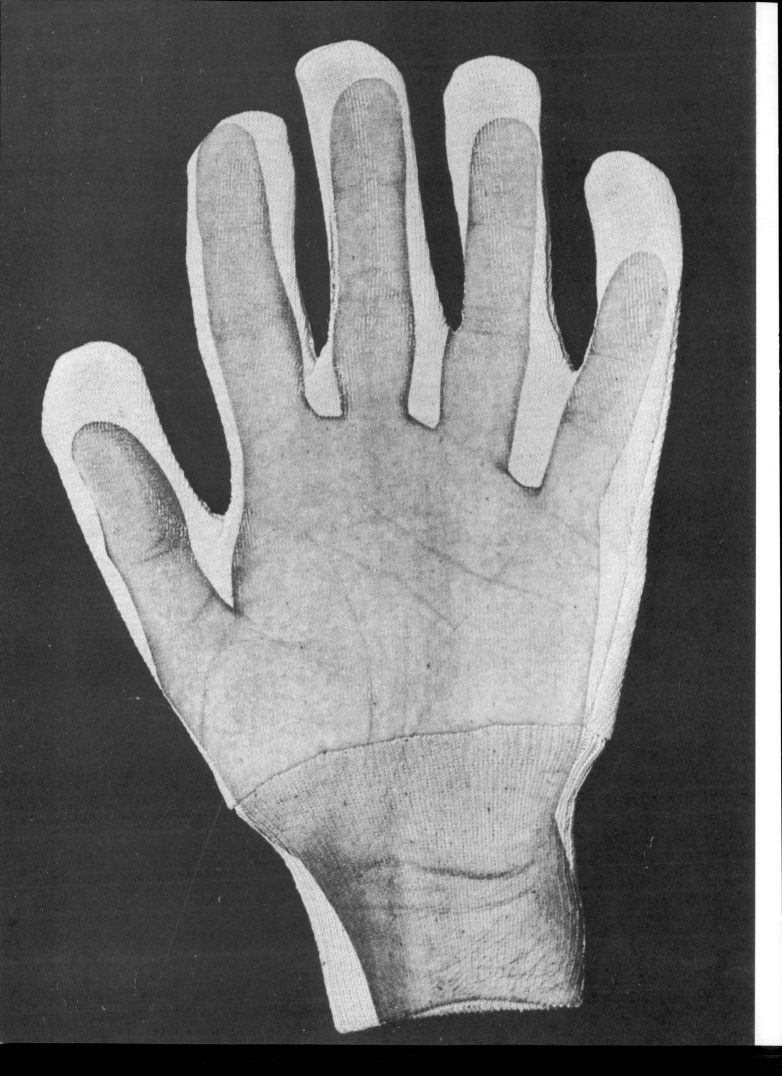

"The Puzzle of the Floating World No. 2," by Katherine Westphal, transfer-printed, quilted, 72″ × 86″.

"Hand on Glove II," by Glen Kaufman, Color Xerox transfer print on cotton, 7″ × 10½″.

"Shroud VII Leaves and Fishes," by M. Joan Lintault,
printed, Color Xerox transfer-printed, sewn, 59″ × 95″.

142

Patchwork effect created by cutting triangles from a variety of printed papers and transferring onto fabric.

Fabric was pleated prior to printing with a master made from strips of printed papers.

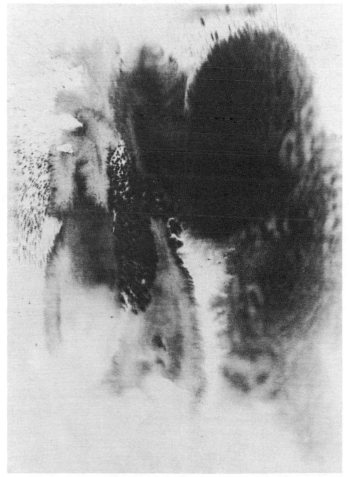
Transfer print on fabric from a paper master that was dampened and sprinkled with disperse-dye grains.

Printed Transfer Papers

Some suppliers stock commercial transfer papers printed with solid colors or patterns. Colors are usually available in a basic palette, and patterns can range from denim and linen-weave effects to polkadots, ginghams, and large-scale designs. These papers are printed with disperse dyes and can be used directly on fabric or applied first to IBM Copier II prints as previously described. A wide range of effects can be achieved through collage, mosaic, and patchwork approaches. A nonaqueous adhesive is best to hold the composition together. Rubber cement on both surfaces is adequate but is affected by the heat. Double-sided transparent tape may be used also. Masking tape is too thick in most instances, and an impression can be transferred into the print on the fabric.

Media Mix

All the above media can be used together to achieve unique effects. All the disperse-dye methods can be incorporated in a single print "master." The "heat-melt" process should always be applied as a last step, as it may be adversely affected by reheating after it has adhered to the fabric surface.

Transfer to Fabric

USING AN IRON

A nonsteam iron is preferred since it has no holes on the sole that could transfer to the finished print. Any iron must be moved about slowly and gently to prevent the shape of the iron from transferring if the size of the design being transferred is larger than the iron. Use a "cotton" setting.

Use a padded printing table, padded board, ironing board (for small pieces), or any flat table that can withstand heat. If a table is used, create a "bed" with flat newspapers. Avoid folds or textures that may be picked up in the print.

Have a supply of newsprint available, as a clean surface is essential. Place a sheet of the newsprint as the heat-transfer base. Place the piece of fabric to be printed on the newsprint with more newsprint on top. Press the fabric between the paper for 10–15 seconds to flatten it and prepare it for printing.

A sample print on all fabric is recommended before attempting a final piece. Test strips can be made easily with any medium (crayon, paste, papers) and quickly tried.

The pressed fabric is left on the clean newsprint, and the transfer paper is placed on top with the dye-covered surface in contact with the fabric. Sometimes pins or tape may help to prevent paper from shifting. Pins or tape should not be in or over the design area or located where they will interfere with the contact and movement of the iron. If the paper is large enough, tape or pins will not interfere with the iron. If the transfer paper is small, pins can be used and moved one at a time to avoid an impression from the pin. Place another piece of clean newsprint over the paper and fabric. The iron should be in contact with the sandwiched layers for 30 seconds to 1 minute or longer. *Gentle* movement is recommended, as a blurred image can result from shifting of the transfer paper. Intensity of color is affected by the length of time the dye is heated. The top layer of newsprint will discolor due to scorching, indicating that the iron is hot enough. Experiment to find the best results.

Commercially printed transfer paper will adhere to the fabric, reducing the problem of blurred images from shifting. The paper can be peeled from a corner to check on the transfer and returned for more heat if necessary. Practice is necessary to achieve an evenly colored print of any size using the printed transfer papers.

"Bran Buds," by Ed Rossbach, Color Xerox transfer print on weft, brocade weave, mixed fibers, 5¾" × 4⅝".

Paper colored with crayons or paste does not adhere to the fabric and thus presents greater problems in getting a clear, sharp print when working with an iron that needs to be moved about.

HEAT PRESS

Working with a dry-mount or transfer press eliminates the problem of shifting paper and the resultant blurred images. The sandwich of newsprint, fabric, transfer paper, and newsprint described above is placed in the press set at 350°–400°F for at least 15 seconds depending on the type of fabric being used. Again, testing is essential. Generally, the time will be less than for an iron since the whole surface is being heated at once.

Additional prints can be made from most transfer-design masters. Occasionally the second and third prints are very similar to the original, especially with directly applied dye paste, as it is usually thicker than printed papers. Most often in the subsequent prints a lighter value or some color change will be seen. Sometimes the dyes will produce different colors on different fabrics.

If large works are attempted, a number of paper masters will be required to cover the surface. As each area is printed and the paper becomes attached to the fabric (especially Color Xerox and commercial transfer paper), leave it in place until the entire surface is printed. Then the papers can be reheated and removed one at a time. Complex designs incorporating a variety of transfer processes can be accomplished in this way.

Since only the dye transfers to the fabric (the thickener is on the paper), where it is fixed by sublimation in the fiber, no further treatment is necessary.

144

"Seven Camels in Search of Treasure," by Katherine West-phal, Color Xerox and crayon transfer on panné velvet, detail of a quilt.

11. Dyes and Pigments

A dye properly chosen and applied will penetrate the fiber and become a part of the fabric. The cloth will retain its natural luster and softness of hand. No one dye will successfully dye all types of fibers or react in the same way to all aftertreatments. The dyer often must sacrifice one attribute for another: brilliance of color may have to be given up to ensure washfastness, or washfastness given up to attain brilliance of color.

Universal fastness tests are used by dye manufacturers for evaluating their colors, and these findings are shown in their catalogues. The craftsman will choose the colors which are most suitable for the conditions and requirements of his own work. It is not necessary to use colors of only one brand. The hue the craftsman prefers may be more washfast in one brand than in another. The method of application will be the same within each class of dyestuff. The differences in formulas given by various manufacturers are usually in the assistants called for. (Often the assistant is sold under a name given by the dye manufacturer.) A list of Chemicals and Assistants are provided at the back of the book.

Fiber Identification

The selection of a dyestuff depends on the fiber content of the fabric to be decorated. If the craftsman does not know the fiber content of a fabric, a simple burning test may be used to identify at least the family group to which it belongs. (It should be noted that cellulosic fibers which have been mercerized are more desirable for dyeing purposes than untreated ones. The chemicals used in the mer-

cerizing process improve the affinity between the fiber and the dye.)

A few threads are unraveled from both warp and weft of the fabric to be identified. They are tested separately by holding with tweezers over a flame long enough to note their reaction.

NATURAL FIBERS. *Cellulosic fibers* (cotton, linen, and viscose rayon) burn readily and continue burning even after the flame is removed. An odor of burning paper is given off.

Protein fibers (silk and wool) burn only while held in the flame. A soft black ash is formed, and an odor of burning hair or feathers is given off.

SYNTHETIC FIBERS. *Acrylic* burns easily, with flame showing a smoky cap, forming a hard black bead. A strong odor difficult to identify is typical.

Nylon does not burn easily but melts away from the flame, forming a hard tan-colored bead. A chemical odor is given off.

Polyester burns slowly and melts, forming a hard black or brown bead. A chemical odor is given off.

Acetate rayon is best identified by placing a small amount of fabric in a jar and covering it with acetone or nail-polish remover. Acetate will dissolve either completely or to a gelatinous mass.

The selection of a dyestuff (or pigment) also depends on the attributes of the various media and the technique to be used in decorating the fabric. The following tables may be of use to the craftsman in making his choice:

Attributes of Media

Medium	Brilliance of color	Washfastness (in lukewarm water)	Boilfastness	Lightfastness (in natural light)
Acid dyes	X	X		X
Disperse dyes	X	X		X
Fiber-reactive dyes	X	X	X	X
Household dyes		X		X
Prepared vat dyes		X	X	X
Pigments	X	X		X

Media, Fabrics, and Methods of Application

Medium	Hot Baths	Cold Baths	Printing Pastes
Acid dyes	S W Nylon		
Disperse dyes	Syn		Syn
Fiber-reactive dyes	C L V	C L V	C L V S W
Household dyes	C L V S W Syn		
Prepared vat dyes		C L V	C L V S
Pigments			C L V S W Syn

Cotton
Linen
Synthetics (nylon, polyester, acetate rayon)
Viscose rayon
Wool

Color Value and Concentration of Dye

Color value when dyeing in a bath (hot or cold) is determined by the amount of dyestuff used in relation to the weight of the fabric being dyed. This value is referred to as depth of shade or depth of dye and is written as a percentage. The following table is offered as a guide to achieving the depth of dye (d.o.d.) desired. Experience is necessary to gain an understanding of dye potentials. (In the table and formulas o.w.f. stands for of weight of fabric.)

Color Value	% of Dyestuff (o.w.f.)
Pale	.5%–1%
Medium	1%–3%
Deep	3%–5%

(Note: To achieve deep values of black and dark blue, 10% d.o.d. is often required.)

COLOR SELECTION

Most classes of dyes are produced in a wide variety of colors to satisfy the specific color needs of the textile industry. Most distributors of dyes to craftspeople, however, are limited by the numbers of dye colors that they can stock. A selection of colors that will provide the widest range should be the goal of the serious surface designer. This can be achieved with the selection of dyes related to the following group of eight: yellow slightly green, yellow slightly orange, red toward blue (cool), red toward orange (warm), blue toward green, blue toward red, brilliant turquoise, and black. These eight colors, with varied intensities and intermixtures, will provide a very wide range of colors.

METRIC MEASUREMENT

Metric measurement is essential to accurate dyeing, since the amounts dealt with are often very small. It is an easily calculated and reliable system, long in use in the sciences and consequently the dye industry. Volumetric measures based on teaspoon, tablespoon, cup, etc., are too cumbersome and unreliable. Gram scales are available in a range of prices. The serious surface designer should invest in a triple-beam balance with a capacity from 0–650 grams. Liter flasks for stock solutions, calibrated glass beakers of 400, 600, and 1000 ml capacity, pipettes with a bulb for measuring small amounts, and graduated cylinders in 50 and 100 ml sizes will all be helpful in working with dyes. (Note: It is essential in working out dye formulas to calculate 1 gram of water as equivalent to 1 milliliter. All other liquids (i.e., acids) will be given the same equivalent.)

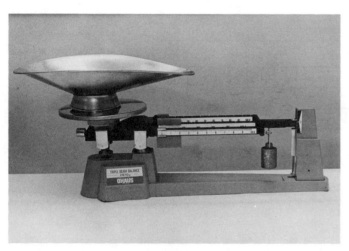

Triple-beam balance with scoop for holding dyes and dry chemicals and counterbalance hanging on right side.

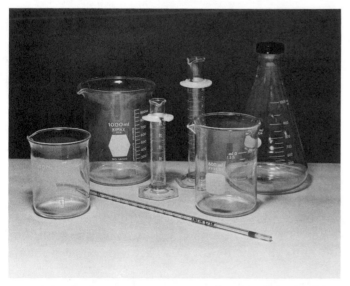

Calibrated beakers, graduated cylinders, pipette, and flask used in metric measurement.

STOCK SOLUTION

Since dye powders consist of very fine particles that are time-consuming to measure in small amounts, it is advisable to prepare a dye stock solution. Measuring is easier, especially when dyeing small amounts of fabric for a pattern book or pale values. A stock solution consists of the dye powder and a given amount of water. Stock solutions can be made up in a variety of concentrations from weak (.2%) to strong (6%). The strength of the stock solution will depend on the type of dyeing to be done and individual experience and preference. For dyeing small fabric samples (i.e., 5 grams) a .2% stock solution is convenient, while a 3% stock solution may work better for larger pieces.

.2% stock solutions (2 g/1)
2 grams dyestuff
1000 milliliters water

3% stock solution (30 g/l)
30 grams dyestuff
1000 milliliters water

The procedure for making the stock solution will vary somewhat depending on the class of dye being used. For dyes used in a cold bath (i.e., reactives) hot tap water is usually adequate to dissolve the dye, while dyes used in hot baths require boiling water.

Place the dye in a glass beaker or other suitable container, paste with a small amount of cold water, then add warm or boiling water as required to dissolve. Bulk the solution to 1000 mls with additional water.

REAGENTS

A reagent is a substance that takes place in or helps bring about a chemical reaction, in this case the dyeing of fiber. The term "assistant" is also applied to these substances. Some reagents are added to the formula based on the weight of fabric, while others are based on the total liquor volume and are called for by g/l (grams/liter). In formulas reagents will be listed as % or g/l.

LIQUOR RATIO

The liquor-to-goods ratio (liquor ratio) is simply a ratio of the total amount of liquid comprising the bath (in grams) to the total amount of fabric (in grams). Long liquor ratios of 20:1 to 40:1 are used for immersion dyeing of fabric. Dyeing of small samples (5 grams) requires a 40:1 ratio to keep the sample covered while stirring it in a bath. If a 5 g sample was being dyed (for a pattern book), 5 g × 40 = 200 g or 200 mls (1g = 1 ml) of liquid are necessary.

The following chart lists the commonly used reagents (assistants) and possible hazards associated with them. Brand names are indicated by an asterisk.

Chemical Name	Common Name	Hazards
Ammonium Hydroxide 5-10%	Ammonia	Very irritating to skin, mucous membranes, and respiratory system. Ingestion of several tablespoons can be fatal. Do not mix with household bleach—together they produce toxic gas.
Ammonium Dihydrogen Phosphate		No hazards are known (a general-purpose food additive).
Sodium Hexametaphosphate	Calgon*	Low toxicity. Ingestion causes nausea, vomiting, and diarrhea.
Sodium Hypochlorite 5%	Clorox*	Corrosive to skin and mucous membranes. Do not use to remove dye from skin. Do not mix with ammonia or vinegar, as the combination produces toxic gas.
	Dispersol* (leveling agent)	Can cause eye burns in concentrated state.
Glacial Acetic Acid	Vinegar (in a dilute state)	Corrosive to skin and can be a respiratory irritant.
Hydrogen Peroxide		Can be irritating to skin, mucous membranes, and eyes.
Sodium Alginate		No known toxicity.
Sodium Bisulfite		Ingestion may cause irritation of the stomach. Inhalation may also cause irritation.
Sodium Carbonate	Sal Soda, Soda Ash, Washing Soda	Corrosive to skin, mucous membranes. Eye irritant. Ingestion causes burns of the mouth, throat, and stomach. Ingestion of large amounts can be fatal.
Sodium Chloride	Salt	Ingestion of large amounts causes vomiting in children.
Sodium Hydrosulfite		Very irritating to eyes, nose, and respiratory system. Ingestion causes moderate stomach irritation. Stored solutions decompose and give off highly irritating sulfur-dioxide gas.
Sodium Sulfate	Glauber's Salt	Ingestion causes diarrhea.
Titanium Dioxide		Ingestion and inhalation can cause slight irritation, which disappears after exposure ends.
Urea		No toxicity known.

SAMPLE FORMULA

The following sample formula for dyeing cotton or viscose rayon with Procion MX dyes will be worked through step-by-step. In the formula 5 grams of cotton are to be dyed at 2% d.o.d. (medium value), utilizing dye in a stock solution.

2% dyestuff (d.o.d.)
35 g/l salt
1.5 g/l sal soda
40:1 liquor ratio

For dyeing small samples a .2% stock solution is recommended. This is achieved by dissolving 2g of dyestuff in 1000 mls water by pasting dye with a small amount of water, adding hot tap water to dissolve, and bulking to 1000 mls. Store this stock solution in a 1 liter flask labeled with the dye color (i.e., Procion Red MX-5B), .2% stock solution, and date (except with the Procion MX series storage of stock solution is not recommended, as the dye reacts with the water and becomes less effective over a period of 24 hours).

To determine the amount of stock solution required, the following formula is followed:

$$\text{Amount of stock solution required} = \frac{\text{(weight of fabric in grams) (d.o.d. in \%)}}{\text{(concentration of stock solution)}}$$

Using this equation for a 2% d.o.d. on 5 gr. fabric with a .2% stock solution, the amount would be determined as follows:

$$\text{Amount of stock} = \frac{(5\ g)\ (2\%)}{.2}$$
$$= 50\ \text{mls dye stock solution}$$
$$.2\%\ (2g/l)$$

If a stock solution was not used, the amount of dyestuff needed would be 2% of 5 g or .1g, a very small amount that would be difficult to weigh accurately.

A liquor ratio of 40:1 is recommended for this size sample. Thus 5g fabric × 40 = 200 mls liquor for the total dyebath (50 mls stock solution plus 150 mls water).

The salt required is 35 g/l (1000 mls); and, since the total bath is 200 mls, the amount of salt required is $^1/_5$ or 7g. The sal soda at 1.5 g/l is calculated in the same manner (divided by 5), equaling .3g.

The formula is now complete for 5g cotton:
  50 mls Procion Red MX-5B stock solution
  7g salt
  .3g sal soda
  200 ml total dyebath

DYE PASTES

In pastes the amount of dyestuff and other components is expressed as parts by weight in relation to 1000 parts of paste. The parts used will be grams with 1000 grams of paste the equivalent of 1000 milliliters in volume (1 liter). If a smaller quantity is needed, the formula can be reduced by a half, a quarter, etc.

Depth of dye or color value will be achieved by the addition of dyestuff to paste in proportions of approximately 5–50 g/l. Specific recommendations will be made for each dye class.

The color value achieved with pigments depends on the amount of extender added to the pigments. No general guides can be given for the proportion to be used because pigments vary greatly. Most manufacturers will suggest the amount of extender to be added; the craftsperson should experiment for the best results.

DYEBATHS

Distilled or deionized water is ideal for dyeing. However, this can be costly, and the dyer can use water softened by a softening system or add Calgon (sodium hexametaphosphate) to the water. The recommended proportion is 4 g of Calgon to 1 l of water.

The amount of water needed in the dyebath can be easily converted from grams to milliliters at a 1:1 equivalent. The amount of water in the dyebath is always based on the weight of the fabric, and the recommended liquor ratio should always be followed. Using less water could result in an uneven uptake of the dye and a streaky or mottled appearance.

Additional dye can be added to the dyebath to adjust the color or increase the value. It should always be added in the form of a solution, after removing the fabric and cooling the bath down to the temperature suggested for the addition of the original amount of dye.

A container large enough to allow free movement of the fabric is necessary for level dyeing or even coloring. In hot and cold dyeing a stainless-steel or enamel container can be used; plastic containers can be used for cold dyeing. Stainless-steel "stock pots" are available from restaurant-supply houses, and enamel preserving kettles or pails may be found in hardware and variety stores.

For hot dyeing the liquor ratio recommended is usually 30:1, except for small samples for pattern books, when 40:1 is recommended. This gives ample space for the movement of dye through the fabric, an important factor in level dyeing. A shorter liquor ratio, as little as 5:1, is used in some cold dyeing. This is referred to as a short dyebath.

Two rules must always be observed in all dyeing: (1) the fabric must be removed from the dyebath before anything is added; (2) after anything is added, the dyebath must be thoroughly stirred before the fabric is returned to the bath.

PATTERN BOOK

It is highly recommended that a pattern book be developed for the dyes that are to be used with regularity. This cannot be done quickly, but it is an important tool and will be an invaluable resource for the designer. Depth of dye has been discussed earlier, and a range of .5%, 2%, and 4% is recommended. For black, dark blue, and other colors desired in very deep values, 10% can be used. Tests on single colors can be conducted on these basic values (d.o.d.) and other intermediates (1%, 3%, 5%, etc.).

Development of the pattern book can proceed from values of a single color to blendings of two or three dye colors and more complex formulations. Common proportions of two colors are: 90% A and 10% B, 80% A and 20% B, 70% A and 30% B, 60% A and 40% B, 50% of each. These proportions make the A color dominant. They can be reversed to make B dominant. The steps can be reduced for a first trial to the 90%–10%, 80%–20%, 60%–40%, 40%–60%, 20%–80%, and 10%–90%.

This makes a convenient group, as the six small dyebaths are the maximum that can be reliably attended at one time, starting groups of three at 10-minute intervals. These color mixtures will be done at a specific d.o.d., with 2% (medium value) a convenient starting point.

Intermixtures of three colors can be based on the following proportions:

Color A	Color B	Color C
60%	20%	20%
40%	40%	20%
40%	20%	40%
20%	60%	20%
20%	40%	40%
20%	20%	60%

A special worksheet has been included as a sample for dyeing with Procion MX (reactive) dyes (Appendix). The same format can be used for other classes of dyes, substituting the correct procedure for the dye being used.

For these tests the dye should be made up in a stock solution for convenience of measuring. The chart showing the amounts of reagents needed (given previously) will also prove helpful.

Dye Tests with Procion MX Dyes

Standard Method   40:1 Liquor Ratio

| Depth of Dye | 5 g fabric | | | 10 g fabric | | |
	Dye Stock Solution	Salt	Sal Soda	Dye Stock Solution	Salt	Sal Soda
.5%	12.5 mls	5g	.3g	25 mls	10g	.6g
2%	50 mls	7g	.3g	100 mls	14g	.6g
4%	100 mls	9g	.7g	200 mls	18g	1.4g
8%	200 mls	11g	.8g	400 mls	22g	1.6g
Bulk to 200 mls				Bulk to 400 mls		

The dyed swatches for the pattern book can be mounted in a looseleaf binder in related color groupings with notations on d.o.d. and color mixtures.

Hot Dyeing

After the fabric is pretreated (see Chapter 4), it must be wet out, or dampened, before it is entered in a hot bath. Most fibers will be damaged if they are exposed to extreme changes of temperature. The fabric should not be plunged into a boiling bath from a cold one or removed from a boiling bath to a cold rinse. It is entered at about 50°C (120°F), and the temperature of the bath is raised gradually. The uptake of most dyes in the hot bath is rapid within the first 15 minutes after the temperature specified in the directions is reached. Thereafter it is gradual, until the fabric will not accept any more. The fabric should be kept under the surface of the dyebath and moved about from time to time to avoid streaking. When the dyeing is finished, the fabric is rinsed several times in baths of progressively cooler water and washed in a soap or detergent bath, then rinsed again and dried.

ACID DYES

The acid dyes recommended for use are those requiring acetic acid (i.e. Ciba Kiton, Keystone Keco, etc.). Stock solutions of acid dyes will keep for several months.

Nylon, Silk, and Wool

Preparation: After thoroughly washing fabric wet out in 10% o.w.f. household ammonia for 1 hour. Rinse thoroughly.

> X% dyestuff
> 15–20% salt o.w.f.
> 6–8% glacial acetic acid 28%*
> 30:1 liquor ratio

(*Glacial acetic acid at 98% can be diluted to 28% concentration by mixing 3 parts acid with 8 parts water.) The higher concentrations of salt and acid are used with deep values of dye.

Method: The dyestuff is pasted in a small amount of cold water and dissolved with boiling water. The bath is prepared with water at 50°C (120°F), and salt is added and dissolved. The acid is added and stirred. The dye solution is added and thoroughly mixed. The wet-out fabric is added and the heat is raised gradually. After 15–20 minutes remove the fabric and add an amount of salt equal to the first addition. After a total of 30 minutes the temperature should be 90°–100°C (195°–212°F). Remove fabric and add an amount of acid equal to the first addition. Return fabric and maintain at 90°–100°C for 30 more minutes. The dye should be "exhausted" by this time and the water clear

(deep values may not totally exhaust). The fabric is rinsed in warm water, washed and rinsed again.

DISPERSE DYES

Polyester

> X% dyestuff
> 20 g/l soap (Ivory Flakes)
> 30:1 liquor ratio

Method: Paste the dyestuff in a small amount of water and add boiling water to dissolve the dye completely. This solution and the soap flakes are added to the bath. Both dye and soap can be prepared in a stock solution and added to the bath. Enter the wet-out fabric and raise the temperature over 15 minutes to 90°–100°C (195°–212°F). Cover the bath to avoid evaporation. Dye at approximately 90°C (195°F) for 1 hour. Rinse and wash as described above.

Acetate, Nylon, Acrylic, Plastics

> X% dyestuff
> 1–2% Dispersol (leveler)
> 1% acetic acid
> 30:1 liquor ratio

Method: Paste and dissolve dye as described above or use stock solution. Do not add to dyebath first. Add leveler and acetic acid to dyebath at 55°C (130°F). Enter wet-out fabric and allow to soak for 5–10 minutes. Remove fabric and add dissolved dye, stirring thoroughly. Gradually bring dyebath to 90°–100°C (195°–212°F) and hold at that temperature for 1 hour. Keep bath covered to avoid evaporation. Rinse and wash in the usual way.

Polyester 2

Polyester is difficult to dye with some disperse dyes without a carrier. Carriers have been noted as possibly hazardous in Chapter 4, and they should be used with great caution in a well-ventilated room. Use the formula for acetate above with the addition of a carrier in the following amounts:

> 6% o.w.f. for pale values
> 9% o.w.f. for medium values
> 12% o.w.f. for deep shades

Method: Follow the method for acetate, adding the carrier with the leveler and acetic acid. Enter the fabric for 5–10 minutes, remove, add dye in solution, return fabric, and continue as indicated above.

REACTIVE DYES

Reactive dyes are classified by their level of reactivity. At one end of the scale are those of low reactivity (Procion H) that require heat for fixation and are more stable in solution, while at the other end are those of high reactivity (Procion MX) that can be fixed without heat, migrate easily, and are not stable in solution for more than 24 hours. The Procion H dyes can be used in a warm bath of 65°–75°C (150°–165°F), and Procion MX can be used in a bath of 50°C (120°F).

Procion H (cotton and viscose rayon)
> X% dyestuff
> 40–100 g/l Glauber's salt
> 20 g/l sal soda (sodium carbonate)
> 30:1 liquor ratio

Glauber's salt is added 40–100 g/l depending on d.o.d.

Depth of Dye	Glauber's salt g/l
less than .5%	40
.5–2%	60
2–4%	80
above 4%	100

Method: The dyestuff is pasted in a small amount of cold water and enough hot tap water is added (not over 75°C) to dissolve the dye. This solution is added to the dyebath at 40°C (105°F). The wet-out fabric is entered and stirred for 10 minutes. One-third of the salt is stirred into the bath at 5-minute intervals; the fabric is removed and reentered for each addition. The bath is stirred and raised slowly to 65°–75°C (150°–165°F) over the next 20 minutes. The sal soda, dissolved in a small amount of hot water, is now stirred into the bath. The fabric is reentered and stirred for about 10 minutes, then stirred every 5 minutes for the next 45 minutes. The fabric is removed from the bath, rinsed in cold water for 15 minutes, simmered in a detergent bath for 15 minutes, and rinsed again in cool water. No further fixation is necessary.

Procion MX (silk)
> X% dyestuff
> 20–30 g/l Glauber's salt
> 2 g/l sal soda (sodium carbonate)

Method: The dyestuff is pasted with a small amount of cold water and dissolved in warm tap water. Prepare the bath at 30°C (85°F); add the dissolved dye and 10 g/l of the Glauber's salt. Stir well and add the wet-out fabric. Add 10–20 g/l Glauber's salt, one-third at a time, over the next 20 minutes, removing the fabric for each addition. Gradually raise the temperature to 50°C (120°F) and hold there for 15 minutes. (Heating the dyebath in a pan of water will help maintain the 50°C temperature.) Add the sal soda, dissolved in hot water. Reenter the fabric and continue dyeing for 40 minutes at 50°C. Rinse the fabric for 15 minutes in cold water

and wash in a detergent bath with 1 g/l sal soda at 80°–90°C (175°–195°F) for 15 minutes. Give a final rinse.

Note: The use of Procion dyes as described above can present some problems in tie-dye. The dyes react with the fiber so readily that all resists must be very secure. It is difficult to retain completely undyed areas: the lightest are usually light tints of the color being dyed. However, satisfactory results have been achieved using both methods in a warm bath as described above.

HOUSEHOLD AND CRAFT DYES
Directions for use are supplied by the manufacturer or distributor.

Cold Dyeing

Some fabric-decoration techniques require cold baths. They are necessary for resist techniques when paste or wax is used to resist the dye. Some classes of dyes are formulated for application in a cold bath regardless of the process being used. When specific temperatures are required, they will be indicated in the method of application.

REACTIVE DYES
Procion MX (long dyebath for cotton, linen, viscose rayon)
(Note: Soft water should be used for the bath. If necessary, add Calgon at 1 g/l.)

> X% dyestuff
> 25–55 g/l salt
> 2–5 g/l sal soda (sodium carbonate)
> 30:1 liquor ratio

The amount of salt and sal soda used will depend on the depth of dye required.

Depth of Dye	Salt g/l	Sal Soda g/l
Up to .5%	25	2
.5–2%	35	2
2–4%	45	4
above 4%	55	5

Method: Paste the dyestuff with a small amount of cold water, then add warm water to dissolve. Add to the dyebath at 30°C (85°F) and stir well. Enter the wet-out fabric and stir for 10 minutes. One-third of the salt is stirred into the bath at 5-minute intervals; the fabric is removed and reentered for each addition. The fabric is moved about in the bath for 20 minutes after the last addition. The sal soda, dissolved in a small amount of hot water, is now stirred into the bath. The fabric is reentered and kept moving about for 10 minutes. The dyeing continues for 30 more minutes, stirring the fabric every 5 minutes. Rinse the fabric in cool water for 15 minutes, *boil* in a detergent bath for 15 minutes, and rinse warm, then cool.

(Note: When dyeing with Procion Turquoise MX-G, Glauber's salt should be substituted for common salt and the temperature of the bath should be raised to 60°C (140°F) 15 minutes after the addition of the sal soda and held there for the remainder of the dyeing.)

Procion MX (short dyebath)

The short dyebath (5:1 liquor ratio) can be used for batik (brushing or sponging over surface), fold-and-dye, and direct application. It is a very concentrated bath with all reagents based on the volume of the liquor.

It is recommended that the Calgon and urea in the following formula be mixed with water as a stock solution. This may be stored indefinitely. The Calgon acts as a water softener and wetting agent while the urea is a swelling agent that aids in dye penetration into the fiber.

> 4 g/l Calgon
> 140 g/l urea
> 1000 mls water

Method: Pour hot water over Calgon and urea and stir until dissolved.

Depth of dye is indicated below as a concentration based on **X** g/l.

Amount of Dyestuff	Color Value
2.5 g/l	Pale
7.5 g/l	Medium
15 g/l	Deep

Method: Paste the dyestuff with a small amount of the stock solution. Add an additional amount, stirring until dye is dissolved. Bulk with additional solution to the volume desired. The dye is activated by the addition of sal soda in the amount of 5 g/l. The dye solution should be used immediately after the addition of the soda. The dyes become less stable and reactive in solution in the presence of soda and should not be used after 24 hours if color reliability is important.

Fixation: Dyes applied in a short dyebath require fixation to form a proper bond with the fiber. A variety of methods can be utilized. All methods are applied before rinsing.

1. The dry fabric is steamed for 5–10 minutes in any available or improvised steam chest.

2. The dry fabric is baked for 5 minutes at 285°F (140°C) in an oven.

3. The dry fabric is ironed for 5 minutes with the iron set at 285°F or at "steam."

4. The dry fabric is tumbled in a laundry dryer set at its hottest setting for 20 minutes. Maximum urea should be used (200 g/l). Check dryer after use for contamination with particles of dye paste.

5. "Batch"-age the wet fabric (covered with plastic, flat or rolled) for 24 hours so that it remains wet. If this method is used, blend 1 part sal soda to 4 parts baking soda. (If a deep value is being dyed, the amount of dye is 15 g/l, so the soda mixture 1:4 could be 3 g/l sal soda and 12 g/l baking soda for a total of 15 g/l.) This method is not recommended if dye can migrate into an undyed area (fold-and-dye).

Washing off: The final treatment consists of rinsing the fabric, fully opened, in cold water for 15 minutes. *Boil* in a detergent bath for 15 minutes and rinse thoroughly.

PREPARED VAT DYES

Sold under the name Inkodye, these prepared vats can be used in a short bath by diluting the paste with water. A ratio of 1:1 will produce a deep value, while 1:5 will provide a pale value. Follow the manufacturer's directions.

Dye Pastes

Dyestuffs must be made into pastes in order to be applied to definite design areas of the fabric. Pastes are required for printing, painting, and other direct techniques of fabric decoration.

The formulas for the pastes contain dyestuff, assistants, and an amount of thickener which may be varied to achieve the consistency needed for a particular use.

Thickeners are made of various gums or starches combined with water. The formulas for thickeners given here are intended as guides. The craftsperson must experiment to find the consistency most useful for the project at hand. The paste should be as thin as possible without actually running beyond the edges of the design areas. A paste which is too thick may deposit excess dye that will migrate outside the design area during fixation. It is more difficult to fix and to wash out during finishing. A very thick paste will also dry too rapidly in the screen and clog the mesh. In general, however, a thin fabric needs a slightly more viscous paste, while a thick fabric needs a thinner one if it is to penetrate the fibers.

Sodium Alginate Thickener

> 10 parts Calgon
> 50 parts sodium alginate grains
> 1,000 parts cold water

Method: The Calgon is dissolved in a small amount of warm water. The cold water is added, and the sodium alginate is sprinkled in while the mixture is stirred briskly so that lumps do not form. The mixture is stirred for 5 or 10 minutes longer and then left for 1 hour, or until it appears smooth and glassy. More water may be added to thin.

Monogum Thickener

50 parts monogum flakes
1,000 parts lukewarm water

Method: The monogum flakes are sprinkled slowly onto the water while stirring briskly with a wire whisk. An electric beater can also be used. Let the mixture stand several hours or overnight until clear and thick. If lumps are seen, strain to remove them. This thickener can be stored for some time with the addition of 1% formaldehyde as a preservative.

DISPERSE DYES (POLYESTER, ACETATE, ACRYLIC, AND NYLON)

7.5 to 15 parts dyestuff
100 parts monogum thickener

Method: Sprinkle the dyestuff on the thickener and mix thoroughly with a wire whisk. The dye tends to thin the thickener, so it should be very stiff before adding the dye. A ratio of 7.5 parts dye:100 parts thickener produces a deep value for most colors. For black and dark blue increase to 15 parts dye:100 parts thickener. Pastes can be stored for some time in the refrigerator. This paste is applied to paper and transferred onto fabric. No fixation or washing out of the fabric is necessary.

REACTIVE DYES

The reactivity of this class of dyes should be considered when choosing one for use in a paste. The Procion MX type is more reactive, can be fixed in the fiber without heat, and is less stable in the paste form. The Procion H type is less reactive, requires heat for fixation, and possesses a very good printing-paste stability (up to 28 days). For this reason the H type is often selected for industrial printing.

Procion MX (cotton, linen, and viscose rayon)

5 to 50 parts dyestuff
50 to 200 parts urea
200 parts hot water
650 parts sodium alginate thickener

The dye is activated by the addition of soda just prior to use:

25 g/l sodium bicarbonate
or
15 g/l sodium carbonate

The following table may be used to determine the amount of dyestuff and urea for the shade desired:

Color Value	Dyestuff	Urea
Pale	5 to 10 parts	50 parts
Medium	10 to 30 parts	100 parts
Deep	30 to 50 parts	200 parts

Method: A stock paste without color is mixed by dissolving the urea in the hot water. This solution is stirred into the thickener. (This paste is usable for several weeks if it is stored in a tightly closed container; it may be kept indefinitely if it is refrigerated.) When the paste is to be used, the dyestuff is added and left to dissolve for 5 minutes. It is then mixed thoroughly. Immediately prior to application the soda is stirred in.

Fixation: As with Procion MX dyes in the short dye-bath, a variety of methods for fixation can be employed.

1. The dry fabric is steamed for 5–10 minutes in any available steamer or steam chest.

2. The dry fabric is baked for 5 minutes at 285°F (140°C) in an oven. If this method is used, the maximum amount of urea, 200 g/l, should be used.

3. The dry fabric is ironed for 5 minutes with the iron set at 285°F or "steam." Maximum urea should be used (200 g/l).

4. The dry fabric is tumbled in a laundry dryer and set at its hottest setting for 20 minutes. Maximum urea should be used (200 g/l). Check dryer after use for contamination with particles of dye paste.

5. Air-dry the fabric in a warm, humid atmosphere for 1 to 2 days.

6. "Batch"-age the damp fabric by covering with plastic for 24 hours. If rolled, the dyed fabric should not touch itself. If this method is used, blend 1 part sal soda and 4 parts baking soda (sodium bicarbonate) in an amount equal to the g/l dye used. (If a deep value is being dyed and the amount of dye is 45 g/l, then the soda mixture at 1:4 would be 9 g/l sal soda and 36 g/l sodium bicarbonate for a total of 45 g/l.)

Washing off: The final treatment consists of rinsing the fully opened fabric in cold water for 15 minutes. Boil in a detergent bath for 15 minutes and rinse thoroughly.

Procion MX (silk)

The formula for printing on silk is the same as for cellulosics, except that sodium bicarbonate should be used and 50 parts urea should be used for all color values. Using less urea will help prevent bleeding or loss of print definition in the steaming.

Fixation: Steaming is recommended for fixation of

silk. The higher temperatures required for dry-heat fixation could be damaging to the silk. About 10 minutes in a dry-steam atmosphere is recommended.

Washing off: The printed fabric, when dry, is rinsed thoroughly in cold water, then rinsed for 5 minutes in water at 60°C (140°F). Treat at 85°C (185°F) for ten minutes in a solution containing 1 g/l sodium carbonate and detergent. Rinse in cool water.

Procion MX (wool—chlorinated is recommended)
    5 to 50 parts dyestuff
    300 parts urea
    10–20 parts sodium bisulfite
    200 parts hot water
    650 parts thickener

The amount of sodium bisulfite is added in relation to the depth of dye:

Parts of dyestuff	Parts of sodium bisulfite
5	0*
5–15	10
over 15	20

*(If no sodium bisulfite is used, add 2 parts acetic acid since the paste must be slightly acidic for wool.)

Method: A stock paste without color is mixed by dissolving the urea in the hot water. This solution is stirred into the thickener. (This paste is usable for several weeks if it is stored in a tightly closed container; it may be kept indefinitely if it is refrigerated). When the paste is to be used, the dyestuff is added and is left to dissolve for 5 minutes. It is then mixed thoroughly. Immediately prior to use the sodium bisulfite or acetic acid is stirred in. It is recommended that the paste be used within 24 hours.

Fixation: The dye is fixed in the fiber by the batch-ageing process. The printed or painted fabric is aged in a damp state by covering with a plastic film for 24 hours. Chlorinated wool will be fixed in a shorter time, but testing is recommended to achieve the best results.

Washing off: The fabric is rinsed in cold water for 5 minutes, then rinsed in water at 60°C (140°F) for another 5 minutes. Treat in water at 60°C (140°F) with 5g/l ammonia for 5–10 minutes to remove excess dye. Enter in a detergent bath at 85°C (185°F) for 10 minutes, then rinse in cool water.

Procion H (cotton, linen, viscose rayon, silk, wool—omit all soda for wool)
    5–50 parts dyestuff
    50–200 parts urea
    200 parts hot water
    650 parts sodium alginate thickener

The dye is activated by the addition of soda just prior to use (except for wool).
    25 g/l sodium bicarbonate
    or
    15 g/l sodium carbonate
(Note: For black use 30 parts sodium bicarbonate or 25 parts sodium carbonate and 50 parts urea.)

The following table may be used to determine the amount of dyestuff and urea for the shade desired:

Color Value	Dyestuff	Urea
Pale	5 to 10 parts	50 parts
Medium	10 to 30 parts	100 parts
Deep	30 to 50 parts	200 parts

Method: A stock paste without color is mixed by dissolving the urea in the hot water. This solution is stirred into the thickener. (This paste is usable for several weeks if it is stored in a tightly closed container; it may be kept indefinitely if it is refrigerated.) When the paste is to be used, the dyestuff is added and left to dissolve for 5 minutes. It is then mixed thoroughly. Immediately prior to application the soda is stirred in. The activated paste may be stored up to 28 days, refrigerated if possible.

Fixation: Use any of the following methods.

1. The dry fabric is steamed for 15 minutes in any available steamer or steam chest. Moist steaming is essential for the fixation of viscose rayon.

2. The following dry-heat processes may be utilized, but urea (200 parts/1000) and sodium carbonate (15 parts/1000) must be used. The dry fabric can be baked for 5 minutes at 285°F (140°C) in an oven; ironed for 5 minutes at 285°F or "steam"; or tumbled in a laundry dryer set at its hottest setting for 20 minutes.

Washing off: The final treatment consists of rinsing the fully opened fabric in cold water for 15 minutes. *Boil* in a detergent bath for 15 minutes and rinse thoroughly.

PREPARED VAT DYES (COTTON, LINEN, VISCOSE RAYON)

Vat dyes ready for use, sold under the brand name Inkodyes, come with complete instructions from the manufacturer. These dyes may be developed and fixed by sunlight, ironing, baking, or steaming.

Resists

REACTIVE DYES

Resists can be printed under reactive dyes that will reserve the color of the ground cloth or deposit a color that will not be affected by subsequent overprinting. Both types require heat treatment after printing the resist and before overprinting with reactive dyes.

White Resist (cotton, linen, viscose rayon)
  500 to 100 parts titanium dioxide
  100 parts Fixapret CP
  650 parts sodium alginate thickener
  10 parts ammonium dihydrogen phosphate
  Bulk with the water to 1000 parts

Method: The titanium dioxide, with a small amount of thickener, is ground to a fine paste with a mortar and pestle to avoid clogging the screen mesh. This paste, along with the Fixapret CP, is added to the thickener. The ammonium dihydrogen phosphate is dissolved in a small amount of water and added to the thickener, which is stirred vigorously to achieve an evenly dispersed mixture. The paste is applied to the fabric, dried as quickly as possible (preferably with a fan), and placed in a laundry dyer set at high temperature for 1 hour. The fabric is then overprinted with Procion dye in one of the methods previously described—including fixation and washoff. Testing with this resist is recommended.

Color Resist (cotton, linen, viscose rayon)
      5–50 parts dyestuff
      850 parts sodium alginate thickener
      100 parts Fixapret CP
      20 parts Catalyst K-20

Method: The dyestuff is added to the thickener, allowed to stand for 5 minutes, and then stirred. The Fixapret and catalyst are mixed together and added to the paste mixture. The paste is applied to the fabric, dried as quickly as possible (preferably with a fan), and placed in a laundry dyer set at high temperature for 1 hour. The fabric is then overprinted with Procion dye in one of the methods previously described, including fixation and washoff. The color resist must be overprinted with a paste containing urea and soda in order to activate the dye in the resist. Testing with this resist is recommended.

PREPARED VAT DYES (COTTON, LINEN, VISCOSE RAYON)

A prepared resist of the cassava type is sold under the brand name Inkodye Resist. Follow the manufacturer's instructions.

Discharge Methods

One method of achieving a light figure on a dark ground is to discharge or remove color from a dark-ground cloth. Cotton, linen, and viscose rayon commercially dyed to deep values are suitable for color discharging in baths of household bleach (Clorox). This method is especially suitable for tie-dye and wax-resist techniques. Bath 2 can also be used to strip color for redyeing.

DISCHARGE BATH 1
      1 part bleach
      3–10 parts water
      30:1 liquor ratio

The concentration of bleach is a matter for consideration and testing. The strongest concentration (1:3) will discharge color faster but will also tend to weaken the fabric. A weaker solution (1:7 or 1:10) may take 30 minutes to 1 hour to discharge the color to the desired value, but there will be less damage to the fabric.

Testing will show that blacks can discharge to browns and tans or to reds; greens can discharge to orange; and blue can discharge to green. A small piece of test fabric can indicate some of the possibilities.

Care should be taken in working with bleach. Work should be carried out in a well-ventilated room and gloves should be worn. Any bleach splashed on the skin should be washed off immediately.

Method: The washed and wet-out fabric is entered in a bath of sufficient volume to allow free movement. The bath should be stirred frequently to assure an even discharge. The action of the bleach can be intensified by heating. The addition of vinegar should be avoided, as it can produce toxic chlorine gas. The bleaching action can be stopped by rinsing in water and then entered in a bath of:
      1 part hydrogen peroxide
      10–20 parts water

The fabric is moved about for 5–10 minutes, rinsed again, washed in a detergent bath, and given a final rinse.

DISCHARGE BATH 2

Sodium hydrosulfite is a color remover that can be used in a discharge bath:
      5–1 g/l sodium hydrosulfite
      30:1 liquor ratio

Method: The wet-out fabric is entered into the bath, and the temperature is raised to 90°C (195°F). The fabric is removed and the hydrosulfite, dissolved in hot water, is added to the bath and thoroughly stirred. The fabric is reentered and moved about until the color is removed. Testing will indicate the proper concentration of hydrosulfite and length of time in the bath. The fabric is removed from the bath, rinsed, and washed in a detergent bath.

COLOR REMOVERS

Household dye manufacturers produce color removers that can be used for discharge or stripping. Follow the directions supplied by the manufacturer. Weaker concentrations of remover to water are suggested for discharge effects.

Pigment Pastes and Inks

There are some pigments in a liquid ink form that can be used for fine brushwork and airbrush applications. These may be thinned to proper consistency by following the directions of the manufacturer.

The craftsman may choose from a number of brands of textile pigments in each of the following classifications: emulsion pigments, synthetic-base pigments, and oil-based pigments. Each brand will be supplied with specific directions and ready-to-use compounds that are combined with the pigment. Among these compounds are extender, transparent base, thinner or reducer, and retarder. An extender is used to add bulk and hardness to the pigment. With some brands the extender is used to produce transparent color, while with others a special transparent base is provided for this purpose. The manufacturer will recommend certain ratios of extender or transparent base to pigment for specific color effects.

Consistency and drying time are factors to be considered in work with pigments. The proper consistency for the technique being used can be achieved by addition of extender and the recommended thinner. If thinner is added, however, the drying time will be shortened, and the pigment may dry in the screen, clogging the mesh. Retarders are usually available to slow the drying time, and experimentation will result in the proper paste mixture.

The emulsion pigments are of special interest for several reasons. Some brands call for water as a thinner and as a solvent for clean-up. This is a great convenience, and it is also less expensive than purchasing solvents such as mineral spirits. The same brands give directions for extenders that the craftsman can mix himself, which is less expensive than purchasing them.

Oil-based printer's inks and block printing inks can be used on fabrics; however, if they are not sold specifically for this purpose, non-fugitive (non-fading) brands should be specified. Two types of white are available in these inks: an opaque cover white and a transparent mixing base. The opaque white is used to produce tints and dense pigments that will cover the ground color of the fabric. The mixing base is used to produce transparent effects similar to those achieved with extender. These pigments are best mixed on a glass or metal palette with a long-bladed metal spatula. If the ink is too thick for proper coating of the brayer, a drop or

two of linseed oil may be added. Too much oil, however, will cause the pigment to bleed when printed, resulting in fuzzy edges.

Fiber-reactive dyes for the Amateur by Dickie Dell Ferro (daughter of the late Meda Johnston)

These formulas and methods are presented for the amateur or beginner. Measurements are given in cups and spoons.

GENERAL CONSIDERATIONS

Tools are the first things you need. Do not use your kitchen utensils. The tools needed are very inexpensive, and the purchase of separate utensils for dyeing is a must. Always wear rubber gloves, and, if you are working with powdered dye, which floats in the air, care should be taken not to breathe it. Wear a mask. (See Chapter 4 for further information on the hazards of dyes.) Use glass, enamel, stainless steel, or plastic tools and pans. You will need measuring spoons, Pyrex measuring cups, and for soaking methods a plastic or stainless pan that will hold at least 2 gallons of dye liquid per pound of fabric, large enough so that the fabric can be stirred without spilling. For the dipping methods small plastic or glass bowls or boxes can be used as your needs dictate. Plastic or stainless ice teaspoons are very helpful. Heavy, large stainless spoons and wood doweling are good for stirring fabrics.

Fabrics most suitable for fiber-reactive dyes are the following, listed in order of suitability: viscose rayon, 100% mercerized cotton, 100% unmercerized cotton, 100% linen, linen and cotton blends, 100% silk, and 100% wool (chlorinated wool is recommended). Silk and wool require different formulas than the other fabrics.

Fabric preparation includes washing before dyeing. Cotton, viscose rayon, and linen are washed in hot water and detergent. Always use liquid or dry detergent that does not contain bleach. You may use your washing machine. Rinse well and dry hanging or in a dryer. This should remove all starch, waxes, or oils. Wash silk and wool in lukewarm water and detergent, rinse well, and hang to dry. Do not use a dryer with wool or silk, The wool will become matted or felted if it becomes too hot or is exposed to rough movement. Sometimes silk will need to be washed more than once. Any finish such as "Wash and Wear" or "Permanent Press" will not take dyeing.

Dye storage is important, as these dyes have a short life after being mixed with water and chemicals. They will become lighter after varying amounts of time, depending on which color and series you are using.

Storing in a refrigerator will somewhat lengthen their life. The dye paste will keep a very long time under refrigeration. The Procion M series dyes should be used within 24 hours. The Procion H series dyes have a longer shelf life and can be stored up to 28 days. Knowing the manufacturer's series numbers helps you in your dyeing, and you should request that your dye supplier furnish you with that information. For example, Yellow MX-4G is an M series dye, and Violet H-3R is an H series dye. In dyeing methods in which you add soda the dye should be used on the same day that it is mixed.

Strength of color is a matter of experimentation and record keeping. That is why a pattern book is so highly recommended. Color value refers to the lightness or darkness of a color. Some colors dye either too dark or too light. By adding or subtracting dye to your formula you can change their values. Especially with some of the dark colors, such as black and navy Procion M series, stronger colors can be obtained by doubling the formula. If that doesn't work, overdyeing should deepen the colors.

FORMULAS

Depending on the technique that you intend to use, you should follow one of the formulas below:

1. Short dyebath—suitable for fold and dye, tie-dye, and brushing or sponging over wax resists (batik)
2. Dye paste—suitable for screen printing, stamping, and direct application with brushes or squeeze bottles
3. Long dyebath—to give a basic color to a length of fabric
4. Yarn dyebath
5. Batik dyebath—for soaking the entire piece after wax resist has been applied
6. Wool and silk dyebath—for adding a basic color to a length of fabric
7. Procion H series dyebaths
8. Wool print paste formulas are given earlier in this chapter

Short Dyebath

Chemicals required:
   Calgon
   urea
   baking soda—bicarbonate of soda

The short dyebath is recommended for fold and dye, tie-dye, and brushing or sponging over wax resist (batik). This dyebath uses a small amount of chemical water and more dye than other formulas. It requires a very short soaking or dipping time. The fabric must not be rinsed until it has been set.

Mix the chemical water first; it can be stored indefinitely:

   1 quart water
   1 teaspoon Calgon
   10 tablespoons urea—increase to 15 tablespoons if using for viscose rayon or setting by tumbling

Color-value measurements per cup of dye liquid vary with the dye color, as some colors are much stronger than others:

Pale: ½ teaspoon per cup of chemical water
Medium: 1½ teaspoons per cup of chemical water
Dark: 2½ teaspoons per cup of chemical water

Once the dye is mixed with chemical water, it begins to age. Wait to mix your dye until you are ready to work. Add a small amount of chemical water to the measured-out dye and work into a paste. When the chemical water is warmed, it helps to dissolve the dye. Now add the remainder of the chemical water and stir. You may have to strain it through a nylon stocking to get out all the lumps.

Baking soda is the last addition:

   1 teaspoon of baking soda per cup of dye liquid

The baking soda causes the dye to start reacting and should be added only to the dye that you plan to use immediately. Adding more soda later will not reactivate the dye. You must mix a new batch every day.

Alternate soda method (does not work for Procion H series dyes): Soak the fabric in a solution of 2 tablespoons washing soda (sodium carbonate) per quart of water, wetting the piece thoroughly. Use gloves to avoid skin irritation. Wring out and hang dry. The dyes mixed with chemical water can now be applied without adding baking soda. The advantage of this method is that the dye mixtures can be used over a longer period of time without deteriorating, since the soda is now in the fabric. Do not set this soda method with dry heat such as ironing, baking, or a clothes dryer, as the soda will cause the fabric to yellow. The steam method or the air-hanging method will best set the dye. After you finish dyeing, hang the fabric to dry in a warm, humid atmosphere. Draw a hot tub of water and hang in the bathroom (with the door tightly closed) for several hours. If the place and time of year are humid and warm, you can hang it outside. Leave the fabric out for several hours.

Setting the dyes, rinsing, and washing are as important as the dye application. Success with reactive dyes cannot be expected unless this part of the process is as carefully carried out as the application. This step causes the dye to become a permanent part of the fabric. The short-dyebath formula must utilize one of the following setting methods.

1. Steaming for 5–10 minutes in a steam kettle or cabinet (see Chapter 4).

2. Baking in a kitchen-type oven for 5 minutes at 285°F. Preheat the oven, place the fabric on a clean, flattish pan, fluff it, and place in the oven. You want the heat to reach all dyed areas of the fabric. This method does not work as well for viscose rayon.

3. Dry-iron. The dry fabric is ironed for 5 minutes, with the iron set at 285°F or on the "steam" setting. Do not put water in the iron, because it often spits and will ruin your work.

4. The dry fabric can be placed in a dryer to tumble at the hottest setting for 20 minutes. Clean the dryer with a damp cloth after use.

5. "Batch" aging process described earlier in this chapter.

For finishing rinse the fabric after it has cooled in a cold-water bath until the water is clear. Open up your fabric so that it won't stain and keep it moving. In this formula one should expect a lot of color to rinse out. Continue rinsing in increasingly warm water until no dye can be seen. Boil in a detergent or liquid-soap bath for 15 minutes and rinse or else wash in a washing machine set on hot with detergent. Dry and iron for the last time.

Dye Paste

    Chemicals required:
    Calgon
    urea
    baking soda—bicarbonate of soda
    sodium alginate

This dye paste is suitable for screen printing, stamping, and direct application with brushes or squeeze bottles. Please note that special instructions are included for use on silk.

Mix the chemical water first; this chemical water can be stored indefinitely:

    1 quart of water
    1 teaspoon of Calgon
    10 tablespoons urea—increase to 15 tablespoons if using for viscose rayon or setting by tumbling

Sprinkle from 1 to 3 teaspoons of sodium alginate over the surface of the chemical water. Stir or shake for 5 or 10 minutes. Allow to sit about 1 hour until completely smooth or glassy on the surface. The amount of sodium alginate depends on the method of application and the type of fabric to be decorated. A thinner paste would be used on a thick fabric, a thicker paste on a thin fabric. A too thick paste can be thinned by adding more chemical water.

Color-value measurements per cup of paste vary with the dye color, as some colors are much stronger than others:

Pale:	½ teaspoon of dye per cup of paste
Medium:	1½ teaspoons of dye per cup of paste
Dark:	2½ teaspoons of dye per cup of paste

Sprinkle the dye powder on the surface of the paste and stir until dissolved.

Baking soda is the last addition:

    1 teaspoon of baking soda per cup of paste

The baking soda causes the dyes to react and should be added only to the dye that you plan to use immediately. Adding more soda later will not reactivate the dye. You must mix a new batch every day.

Setting the dyes, rinsing, and washing are as important as the application. Success with reactive dyes cannot be expected unless this part of the process is carefully carried out. This step causes the dye to become a permanent part of the fabric. The dye-paste formula must utilize one of the following methods of setting the dye before rinsing.

1. Steaming for 5–10 minutes in a steam kettle or cabinet (see Chapter 4).

2. Baking in a kitchen-type oven for 5 minutes at 285°F. Preheat the oven, place the fabric on a clean, flattish pan, fluff it, and place it in the oven. The heat should reach all dyed areas of the fabric. This method does not work well for viscose rayon.

3. Dry iron. The dry fabric is ironed for 5 minutes over all the areas that have been dyed, with the iron set at 285°F or on a "steam" setting. Do not put water in the iron, because it often spits and will ruin your work.

4. The dry fabric can be placed in a dryer to tumble at the hottest setting for 20 minutes. Clean the dryer with a damp cloth after use to remove any dye residue.

5. "Batch" aging process described earlier in this chapter.

For finishing rinse the fabric after it has cooled in a cold-water bath until the water is clear. Open up your fabric so that it won't stain and keep it moving. In this formula it is sometimes hard to rinse the paste but don't give up. Continue rinsing in increasingly warm water until no dye can be seen. Boil in a detergent or liquid-soap bath for 15 minutes and rinse or else wash in a washing machine set on hot with detergent. Dry and iron for the last time.

For silk the formula is the same except that steaming is recommended for setting the dye. Hang-dry the fabric and then steam for 10 minutes. A dry-heat-setting method might damage the silk. Rinse the fabric in cold water until the rinse water is clear. Soak the silk in a warm soap bath with 1 teaspoon of baking soda. Give it a final rinse and hang-dry. Do not tumble-dry silk.

Long Dyebath

Chemicals required:

Calgon

table or common salt

washing soda or sal soda

The long dyebath is used to give a length of fabric a basic allover color. This formula should dye 2 to 4 yards of 36″ medium-weight fabric or about 1 pound. Use about 1 teaspoon Calgon per quart water to soften if you have hard water.

The color-value measurements are given per pound of fabric:

Pale: ¼ teaspoon per pound of fabric
Medium: ½ teaspoon per pound of fabric
Dark: 1 teaspoon per pound of fabric

Mix the dye into a smooth paste with a small amount of water, add more water, and work into liquid. Stir the dye into a plastic, enamel, or stainless-steel pan containing 3 gallons of water per pound of fabric.

Dampen the fabric in clear water, squeeze, and enter it into the dyebath. Stir gently for 10 to 15 minutes. Add the salt to the bath. Always remove the fabric when making any addition to the bath. Always stir the liquid before returning the fabric to the bath. Measure the salt into 3 equal parts and add to the bath separately (removing the fabric each time), with 5 minutes between additions:

3 tablespoons salt for a pale color
6 tablespoons salt for a medium color
9 tablespoons salt for a dark color

Continue stirring for 20 minutes. Remove fabric and add:

3 tablespoons of washing soda

Dissolve it in a small amount of hot water. Return the fabric to the bath and dye for 1 hour longer, stirring from time to time. Stirring keeps the fabric from streaking. Rinse the fabric and give it a hot soap bath.

Yarn Dyebath

Use the long dyebath for cotton and linen yarn dyeing. Use the short dyebath for tie-dyed warp. For tie-dyeing try spooning or squeeze-bottling the dye if it creeps too far under your ties. Use the dye paste for stamping or brushing a design on the warp before weaving. Slide a padded drawing board under the warp for better control. For wool or silk yarns use the wool and silk dyebath.

Batik Dyebath

Chemicals required:

Calgon

common or table salt

washing soda or sal soda

The batik dyebath is used for a fabric that has been wax-resisted or batiked and for which you want an allover dye. The washing soda causes the wax to disintegrate somewhat; more beeswax than paraffin is recommended for the wax mixture. This formula will dye about 2 yards of fine cotton fabric. It will not be enough for 2 yards of velveteen. For larger or heavier pieces enlarge the amounts accordingly; for smaller ones divide the formula, which for about 1 pound of fabric before resist is applied.

The color-value measurements are given here per pound of fabric before waxing:

Pale: ½ teaspoon dye per pound of fabric
Medium: 1 teaspoon dye per pound of fabric
Dark: 2 teaspoons dye per pound of fabric

Make a paste of the dye with a small amount of lukewarm water. Add a teaspoon of Calgon to each quart of water if you have hard water. Continue adding water until 2 cups have been mixed with the dye. Strain through a nylon stocking if lumpy. In a glass, stainless-steel, or plastic container dissolve completely 6 tablespoons of salt in 1 quart of hot water. Allow to cool. When cool, mix in the dye liquid.

Dampen the waxed fabric, squeeze out excess water, and enter into the dyebath. Turn in the bath continuously for 6 minutes. Dissolve 2 level tablespoons of washing soda in ¼ cup boiling water. Remove fabric from the dyebath and add the soda water. Stir. Return the fabric to the bath and dye for 15 minutes, turning occasionally. Rinse in cold water until no dye shows in the rinse water. Dry and wax again until the design is complete. Dry, rinse, and dry for the last time.

To iron out the wax, place the fabric between several layers of paper. Do not use freshly printed newspaper, as the print can come off onto your fabric. Iron out all the wax until no more comes off on the paper. The last vestiges are removed by washing the fabric in a hot detergent bath and rinsing it in cold water several times. Your local dry cleaner's may be able to clean it for you.

Wool and Silk Dyebath

Chemicals required:

Calgon

table or common salt

vinegar or glacial acetic acid

This formula gives a basic color to a length of fabric or yarn. It will color 2 to 4 yards of 36″ medium-weight fabric or 1 pound fabric or yarn.

Color-value measurements per pound of fabric or yarn:

Pale: ½ teaspoon of dye per pound of fabric or yarn

Medium: 1 teaspoon of dye per pound of fabric or yarn
Dark: 2 teaspoons of dye per pound of fabric or yarn

Mix the dye into a smooth paste with a small amount of warm water. Add 1 teaspoon Calgon per quart if you have hard water. Add more water and work into a liquid. Strain through a nylon stocking if necessary into a bath of enough water to cover the fabric so that it will move about loosely. Allow about 3 gallons per pound of fabric. Add salt in the proportions of:

3 tablespoons of salt for a pale color
6 tablespoons of salt for a medium color
9 tablespoons of salt for a dark color

Dampen the fabric or yarn in clean water, squeeze out excess water, and enter into the dyebath. Heat the dyebath to a gentle simmer, allowing about 45 minutes. Move the fabric or yarn very gently in the liquid. When the bath begins to simmer, leave it for 10 minutes. Remove the fabric and add 1 cup of vinegar or 4 tablespoons glacial acetic acid. Stir. Return the material to the bath and simmer another 10 minutes. Remove from heat and allow the fabric to cool in the bath very gradually. Wool will mat if subjected to violent changes of temperature or to violent agitation. When completely cool, remove from dyebath, rinse out excess dye well, give it a cool soap bath, rinse, and hang to dry. Do not use a tumble dryer.

Procion H Series Dyebaths

These dyes have a longer storage life but need special directions.

1. For the long dyebath the bath should be kept at a simmer for the entire process. Do not enter a cold fabric into a hot bath. Rinse in warm water before entering into the simmering dyebath. Color results are sometimes unpredictable.

2. For the short-dyebath and dye-paste formulas add 3 teaspoons of baking soda per cup of dye liquid. For setting use a steaming method.

3. For batik use the short-dyebath formula and triple the amount of baking soda. Brush or sponge the soda on. Do not use the batik-bath formula. For the batik or wax-resist method iron out as much of the wax as possible, steam, then rinse and wash.

APPENDIX

Pattern Book Worksheet

Dye _____   Date _____

Fiber _____   Weight of Sample _____

Test #   Color A _____   Color B _____   Color C _____

_____   _____ % _____ mls   _____ % _____ mls   _____ % _____ mls

_____   _____ % _____ mls   _____ % _____ mls   _____ % _____ mls

_____   _____ % _____ mls   _____ % _____ mls   _____ % _____ mls

If color mixture, d.o.d. _____ .

Procedure for dyeing with Procion MX dyes

Time

1. Prepare liquor of stock solution and water at 45°C.
2. Add hot water to sal soda and stir to dissolve.

Begin _____
3. Add wet fabric and stir for 10 mins.
_____
4. Remove fabric.
5. Add ⅓ of salt and stir to dissolve.
6. Return fabric, stir 5 min.
_____
7. Remove fabric, add ⅓ more salt, and stir to dissolve.
8. Return fabric, stir 5 min.
_____
5. Remove fabric, add remaining salt, and stir.
10. Return fabric and stir 20 min.
_____
11. Remove fabric and add sal soda solution.
12. Return fabric and stir 10 min.
_____
13. Stir every 5 min. for 30 additional mins. (For Procion turquoise MX-G raise temperature of bath to 60°C (140°F), enter fabric, and dye last 20 min.)
_____
14. Remove and rinse in cool water 15 min.
_____
15. Boil in water and detergent 15 min.
_____
16. Rinse in warm, then cool water 15 min.

CHEMICALS AND ASSISTANTS

A variety of assistants and other chemicals are called for in the formulas given for dyebaths, dye pastes, and thickenings. A number of chemicals are also required for pretreatments and aftertreatments of fabrics. Most are available at local pharmacies or drug-supply houses. A few are sold under brand names; these are indicated by an asterisk.

Acetic acid is an exhausting agent used with several dyestuffs. The concentrated, or glacial, type is usually required. Vinegar is a weak form of acetic acid.

Ammonium dihydrogen phosphate is used in resist pastes with fiber-reactive dyes to help resist subsequent dyeing.

Calgon* (sodium hexametaphosphate) is a water softener.

Carrier acts as a swelling agent when dyeing polyester fiber with disperse dyes.

Catalyst K-20* is used in resist pastes with reactive dyes when a color is included in the paste.

Common salt (sodium chloride) creates an affinity between several dyestuffs and fibers. It acts as a retardant with some dyestuffs.

Fixapret CP* is used in resist pastes with fiber-reactive dyes.

Glauber's salt creates an affinity between several dyestuffs and fibers. It acts as a retardant with some dyestuffs.

Sodium bicarbonate is required for the fixation of fiber-reactive dyes.

Sodium bisulfite is used in the application of some reactive dyes to wool.

Sodium carbonate (sal soda, soda ash, washing soda) is the alkali essential for the fixation of reactive dyes in some applications.

Sodium hydrosulfite is a bleaching agent.

Sodium sulfoxylate formaldehyde is used in discharge pastes.

Synthetic detergents (household liquid detergents) are required in the use of several dyestuffs.

Titanium dioxide is used in resist pastes with reactive dyes to secure a good white.

Urea is a swelling agent used with reactive dyes.

GLOSSARY

Aftertreatment—Any process a fabric may require after the application of dye, such as fixation and finishing.

Assistant—Chemical that aids in creating the bond between dye and fiber.

Batik—Technique of decoration in which hot wax is applied to the fabric to resist subsequent coloring.

Binder—Substance in which pigments are suspended to make a paste.

Bleeding—Running of color from a dyed fabric when dampened.

Blockout—Substance used to fill the mesh of a screen to prevent passage of the printing medium in screen printing.

Block Printing—Technique of decoration in which the fabric is printed by hand with wood or linoleum blocks.

Butt Joint—Method of printing repeats so that they meet along a straight line.

Carrier—An assistant that aids in the penetration of dye into the fiber.

Cellulosic Fiber—Fiber obtained from a plant, such as cotton or linen.

Cockle—The wrinkling that occurs when paper absorbs moisture.

Cold Dyeing—Process of coloring fabric in a bath at about 40°C (100°F).

Color Separation—Procedure by which the various colors of a design are isolated for printing one at a time.

Crackle—Fine-line effects produced in the wax-resist technique.

Depth of Dye (d.o.d.)—The value of the dye color on the fabric. Also expressed as Depth of Shade (d.o.s.).

Discharge—Removal of some or all of the color from a fabric.

Discharge Paste—Paste containing a bleaching substance for removing color from a fabric.

Dovetail Joint—Method of printing repeats so that a portion of one unit fits into a part of the next without touching it.

Dyebath—Solution of dyestuff, assistants, and water in which fabrics are colored.

Dye Paste—Viscous mixture of dyestuff, chemicals, and thickener used to color fabrics in printing and painting techniques.

Dyestuff—Material that colors fabrics by combining chemically with the fiber.

Dye Uptake—Absorption of the colorant by the fiber.

Exhaust—To cause total absorption of color from a dyebath by the fiber.

Exhausting Agent—Chemical which promotes the absorption of color from the dyebath by the fiber.

Extender—Paste used to reduce the color value of a dye or pigment paste.

Fastness—Ability of a dye or pigment to withstand washing, boiling, or exposure to light.

Finishing—Process of washing, rinsing, and ironing decorated fabrics.

Fixation—Process by which colors are permanently fixed in or attached to the fiber of a decorated fabric.

Flock—Finely shredded fiber used to give an absorbent surface to wood and linoleum blocks.

Ground Color—The color of a predyed fabric receiving further decoration. The term Blotch is also used to identify the ground color of a printed fabric.

Hot Dyeing—Process of coloring fabric in a heated bath.

Immersion Dyeing—Process of coloring a fabric in which the fabric is submerged in the bath.

Level Dyeing—Even coloring of a fabric.

Leveler—An assistant that aids in the even uptake of dye into fabric.

Liquor Ratio—Amount of water in a dyebath in relation to the weight of the fabric to be dyed.

Mercerizing Process—Finishing process used for cotton goods to increase their luster and strengthen and improve their affinity with dyes.

Migration—Spreading of color outside the area of application.

Mordant—Substance which creates an affinity between dye and fiber.

Of Weight of Fabric (o.w.f.)—A term used to express a relationship between reagents or liquid to fabric weight.

Overdyeing—Dyeing over previously dyed areas with another color.

Overlapping Joint—Method of printing repeats in which a portion of one unit overlaps a portion of the next unit.

Overprinting—Printing over previously printed areas with the same or another color.

Pattern Book—Collection of samples of dyed fabric with formulas and technical information.

Permanent Blockout—Stencil material, not affected by the printing medium, used to fill the mesh of a screen to prevent passage of the medium in screen printing.

Pigment—Material that colors fabric by coating the fiber.

Pretreatment—Any process by which fabric is prepared for the application of dye.

Reagent—A substance that takes place in or brings about a reaction (Assistant).

Reducer—See Thinner.

Registration—Exact alignment of one repeat with another in printing.

Registration Mark—Visible indicator used as a guide in printing.

Remover—Liquid used to clean a stencil material from a screen in screen printing.

Repeat—Basic unit of design in fabric decoration.

Resist—Process or material which prevents dye from reaching designated areas of a fabric.

Retardant—Chemical that delays the absorption of dye by a fiber.

Screen Printing—Technique of decoration in which color is forced onto the fabric through a stencil attached to a screen made of fabric stretched on a frame.

Size—Substance applied to fabric to give it added strength or body.

Solvent—Liquid used to remove stencil materials in screen printing and dissolve media for cleanup.

Squeegee—Tool with a wooden handle and a rubber blade used to force the printing medium through the mesh of a screen in screen printing.

Stamping—Means of transferring a design to fabric by pressing a color-coated object onto its surface.

Stencil—Thin material perforated with a design through which a printing medium is forced onto the fabric to be decorated.

Stiffness of Hand—Inflexibility of fabric to the touch.

Stock Solution—A solution of dye or assistant in a specified ratio to water (g/l).

Straight of the Weave—Following the warp or weft threads of a fabric.

Stripping—Removal of color from a dyed fabric by a chemical means.

Synthetic Fiber—Fiber produced by chemical synthesis.

Temporary Blockout—Stencil material used to fill the mesh of a screen in areas subsequently to be opened to permit passage of the printing medium in screen printing.

Thickener—Substance made with a gum or starch and added to dye pastes to achieve the consistency needed for application to a fabric.

Thinner—Liquid used to thin the consistency of a dye or pigment paste.

Tie-dye—Technique of decoration in which the fabric is bound so it will resist color in designated areas.

Transfer Printing—A process whereby pattern or color is transferred from paper to fabric with the application of heat.

Warp—Longitudinal yarns in woven fabric.

Weft—Crosswise yarns in woven fabric.

Wet out—To thoroughly dampen fabric before dyeing.

SUPPLIERS

Advance Process Supply Co.
400 North Noble Street
Chicago, Illinois 60622
All screen-printing supplies,
  pigments

Aiko's Art Materials
714 North Wabash Avenue
Chicago, Illinois 60611
Wax tjantings, rice and starch paste
  ingredients, dyes

Apple Room
510 N. Hoover Street
Los Angeles, California 90004
Vat dyes, Inkodyes, batik supplies

BASF Wyandotte Corp.
100 Cherry Hill Road
Parsippany, New Jersey 07054
Fixapret CP and other chemicals

BASF Wyandotte Corp.
491 Columbia Avenue
Holland, Michigan 49423
Dyes and pigments

Bona Venture Supply Co.
#17 Village Square
St. Louis, Missouri 63042
Airbrushes and supplies, dyes,
  special fugitive fabric markers
  and pencils

Cerulean Blue, Ltd.
1314 N. E. 43rd Street
Seattle, Washington 98105
Procion reactive, disperse, napthol,
  Deka, Ciba vat and acid dyes,
  Versatex pigments, fabrics,
  chemicals, and batik supplies

Cincinnati Screen Process
  Supplies, Inc.
1111 Meta Drive
Cincinnati, Ohio 45237
Screen-printing supplies, pigments

Colonial Printing Ink Co.
183 E. Union Avenue
East Rutherford, New Jersey 07073
Textile inks, screen printing
  supplies

Craftools, Inc.
1 Industrial Road
Woodbridge, New Jersey 07075
Wax, tjantings, stretchers

Dadant and Sons, Inc.
Hamilton, Illinois 62341
Beeswax in large amounts

Dharma Trading Co.
P. O. Box 916
San Rafael, California 94902
Procion dyes, fabrics, tjantings,
  wax, thickener

D.Y.E. Textile Resources
3763 Durango Avenue
Los Angeles, California 90034
Procion reactive, acid, disperse
  and Deka dyes, chemicals,
  fabrics, batik supplies

Fab/Dec
3553 Old Post Road
San Angelo, Texas 76901
Procion fiber-reactive dyes,
  sodium-alginate thickener,
  fabrics, urea

Fibrec, Inc.
P. O. Box 985
San Francisco, California 94101
Reactive dyes, pigments, batik
  supplies

Flynns
Box 11304
San Francisco, California 94101
Mail order catalog of dyes
  and textile art supplies

Hilton-Davis Chemical Co.
P. O. Box 1117
Greenville, South Carolina 29611
Seabond colors (pigments)

ICI Americas, Inc.
Concord Pike & New Murphy Road
Wilmington, Delaware 19899
Procion dyes

Industrial Rubber and
  Safety Products, Inc.
1840 New Savannah Road
P. O. Box 6306
Augusta, Georgia 30906
3-M respirators

Ivy Craft Imports
6806 Trexler Road
Lanham, Maryland 20801
Sennelier (France) Gutta resist and
  dyes, steamers, batik supplies

Keystone Aniline & Chemical Co.
321 North Loomis Street
Chicago, Illinois 60607
Variety of dyes

The Naz-Dar Company
1087 N. North Branch Street
Chicago, Illinois 60622
All screen-printing supplies,
  pigments for printing

Norton Company
Safety Products Division
2000 Plainfield Pike
Cranston, Rhode Island 02920
Respirators

Pylam Products Co.
95–10 218th Street
Queens Village, New York 11429
Reactive and other dyes, pigments

Rupert, Gibbon and Spider
470 Maylin Street
Pasadena, California 91105
Deka colors, pigments

Screen Process Supplies
  Manufacturing Co.
1199 E. 12th Street
Oakland, California 94606
Inkodyes, screen-printing and batik
  supplies

Siphon Art
74-D Hamilton Drive
Ignacio, Califorina 94947
Versatex pigment, Dorland's liquid
  wax resist

Test Fabrics, Inc.
P. O. Drawer O
200 Blackford Avenue
Middlesex, New Jersey 08846
Wide variety of fabrics for surface
  design

Thai Silks
252 State Street
Los Altos, California 94022
Wide variety of silk fabrics

BIBLIOGRAPHY

Albeck, Pat. *Printed Textiles*. London, Oxford University Press, 1969.

American Fabrics Magazine (eds.). *Encyclopedia of Textiles*. Englewood Cliffs, New Jersey: Prentice-Hall Inc., 1960.

Anderson, Donald M. *Elements of Design*. New York: Holt, Rinehart & Winston, 1961.

Ballinger, Louise B., and Vroman, Thomas F. *Design: Sources and Resources*. New York: Reinhold Publishing Corp., 1965.

Barazani, Gail Coningsby. *Safe Practices in the Arts and Crafts: A Studio Guide*. New York: College Art Association, 1978.

Beitler, Ethel Jane, and Lockhart, Bill. *Design For You*. New York: John Wiley and Sons, Inc., 1961.

Belfer, Nancy. *Designing in batik and tie dye*. Worcester, Massachusetts: Davis, 1972.

Bhushan, Jamila B. *The Costumes and Textiles of India*. Bombay: D. B. Taraporevala & Sons, 1958.

Bird, Junius. *Paracas Fabrics & Nazca Needlework*. Washington, D.C.: National Publishing Co., 1954.

Birren, Faber. *Creative Color*. New York: Reinhold Publishing Corp., 1961.

Born, W. "Textile Ornament," *Ciba Review #37*. The Society of Chemical Industry in Basle, January, 1941.

Brief Guide to Oriental Painted, Dyed and Printed Textiles. London: Victoria and Albert Museum, H. M. Stationary Office, 1950.

Briggs, Asa (ed.). *William Morris Selected Writings and Designs*. Baltimore: Pelican Books, 1962.

Bystrom, Ellen. *Creating with Batik*. New York: Van Nostrand Reinhold, 1974.

Chiasson, Constance M. "Textile Dyeing the Black Art," *Surface Design Journal*, Spring 1979.

Clarke, W. *An Introduction to Textile Printing*. London: Newnes-Butterworths, 1977.

Collier, Graham. *Form, Space and Vision*. Englewood Cliffs, New Jersey: Prentice-Hall Inc., 1963.

Conran, Terence. *Printed Textile Design*. London: The Studio Publications, 1957.

The Cooper Union Museum Chronicle, Vol. 3, No. 5 (October 1963).

Design by the Yard, Textile Printing from 800–1956. New York: The Cooper Union Museum, 1956.

D'Harcourt, Raoul. *Textiles of Ancient Peru and Their Techniques*. Seattle: University of Washington Press, 1962.

Emerson, Sybil. *Design: A Creative Approach*. Scranton: International Textbook Co., 1955.

Erickson, Janet. *Block Printing on Textiles*. New York: Watson-Guptill Publications, 1961.

Halpern, Fay and McCann, Michael. "Health Hazard Report: Caution with Dyes," *Craft Horizons*, August 1976.

Hunter, George L. *Decorative Textiles*. Philadelphia: J. B. Lippincott Co., 1918.

ICI Ltd. Dyestuffs Division. *An Outline of the Chemistry and Technology of the Dyestuffs Industry*. Birmingham: ICI, 1968.

———. *Procion Dyestuffs in Textile Dyeing*. Great Britain: Imperial Chemical Industries Dyestuffs Division, 1962.

Jacobson, Egbert. *Basic Color*. Chicago: Paul Theobald, 1948.

Jenkins, C. L. "Textile Dyes are Potential Hazards," *Journal of Environmental Health*. Vol. 40, No. 5 (March/April 1978).

Joseph, Marjory L. *Introductory Textile Science*. New York: Holt, Rinehart & Winston, 1966.

Kosloff, Albert. *Screen Process Printing*. Cincinnati: The Signs of the Times Publishing Co., 1958.

Krevitsky, Nik. *Batik: Art and Craft*. New York: Reinhold Publishing Corp., 1964.

Kümpers, Hilde. *Kunst auf Baumwolle*. Dortmund: Ardey-Velag, 1961.

Langewis, Laurens, and Wagner, Fritz A. *Decorative Art in Indonesian Textiles*. Amsterdam: Uitgeverij C.P.J. Van der Peet, 1964.

Larsen, Jack Lenor. *The Dyer's Art: Ikat, Batik, Plangi*. New York: Van Nostrand Reinhold, 1976.

Maile, Anne. *Tie and Dye*. London: Mills & Boon Ltd., 1963.

Means, Philip Ainsworth. *A Study of Peruvian Textiles*. Boston: The Museum of Fine Arts, 1932.

Nelson, George. *Problems of Design*. New York: Whitney Publications, 1957.

Nihon Sen'i Isho Senta. *Textile Designs of Japan*, Vol. I (1959) and Vol. III (1961). Osaka: Japan Textile Color Design Center.

Osumi, Tamezo. *Printed Cottons of Asia*. Tokyo and Rutland, Vermont: Bijutsu Shuppan-Shu and Charles E. Tuttle, 1963.

Percival, MacIver. *The Chintz Book*. New York: Stokes Co., n.d.

Pettit, Florence Harvey. *America's Printed and Painted Fabrics, 1600–1900*. New York: Hastings, 1970.

Proctor, Richard M. *The Principles of Pattern*. New York, Van Nostrand Reinhold Company, 1969.

Proud, Nora. *Textile Printing and Dyeing*. New York: Reinhold Publishing Corp., 1965.

Röttger, Ernst. *Creative Paper Design*. New York: Reinhold Publishing Corp., 1961.

Russ, Stephen. *Fabric Printing by Hand*. New York: Watson-Guptill Publications, 1965.

Sax, N. Irving. *Dangerous Properties of Industrial Materials*. New York: Van Nostrand Reinhold, 1975.

Simmons, Max. *Dyes and Dyeing*. Australia: Van Nostrand Reinhold, 1978.

Trowell, Margaret. *African Designs* (2nd ed.). New York: Frederick A. Praeger, 1966.

INDEX